MERRY CHRISTMAS

Amanda Jantzi

New Harbor Press

RAPID CITY, SD

Jantzi/New Harbor Press
1601 Mt Rushmore Rd, Ste 3288
Rapid City, SD 57701
www.NewHarborPress.com

Merry Christmas / Jantzi. -- 1st ed.
ISBN 978-1-63357-445-8

To the Giver of Words and Dreams. May this story be used to further the kingdom of Christ. All glory be to You.

To my sister Lori, the underpaid critic, editor, supporter, listening ear, and best friend. Merry Christmas.

And to you, the reader. May you discover that God makes all things beautiful—in His time.

CHAPTER ONE

It was Saturday, which meant Cole Greyson had to put a little silver ball on the top of each tree his friend Stephanie Walker piped onto the round, cutout cookies. *Talk about tedious—especially when I'd rather eat the cookie,* Cole thought.

Aunt Sue had been delighted to start her own bakery. He stuck up for her. It kept them busy and provided needed income. Cole would stand up for his aunt any day. After all, it was Aunt Sue who had given him a home. She had opened her heart to him after the accident that had claimed his parents and his gratitude ran deep.

"Hey, Cole! You better stop daydreaming. You're falling behind," Stephanie teased.

Sure enough, he was twenty cookies too slow. Cole quickened his pace and got icing on his fingers. *Great.*

While he washed his hands the door flew open, bringing a gust of chilly December air with it. His cousin Tomika Woods hurried in, dragging Kelsi Graham along behind her.

"Cole, you'll never guess what Kelsi did," Tomika panted.

Cole couldn't tell if she was scared, excited, angry, or flustered. Actually, it was probably a mixture of all four. That didn't surprise him. Tomika regularly got worked up over small things. Cole had heard firsthand stories from her brother Tyrell and had witnessed a couple of incidents himself. Having Tyrell for a brother probably didn't help the problem. Tyrell could talk too much at times, but Cole knew he could trust him with his most secret thoughts. Aunt Sue often said they could pass as brothers with their dark hair and blue eyes, but the resemblance stopped there. Personality-wise they were much different. Tyrell was more impulsive yet easygoing. Cole was considered serious and quiet. That shocked him when he first heard it because inside he sure didn't feel "serious and quiet." After all, what fifteen-year-old does? Although right now Tomika's indignation had him feeling a little serious.

"What's up?" Cole asked picking up the container and fishing out another silver ball. He noticed Kelsi looked worried. "Is Jupiter on a collision course with the Earth?"

"Of course not," Tomika exclaimed. "Kelsi told Pastor Jordan we'd take care of the Christmas Event this year!"

"He asked," Kelsi defended herself.

The Christmas tree suffered an unexpected jab. Cole barely noticed the icing on his fingers. "You said WHAT?!"

The Christmas Event was held annually at the Living Free Church where Cole attended. Usually, an older couple would show slides or the choir would be asked to give a program. Anyone could volunteer and, obviously, Kelsi had dropped a big hint without asking the rest of her friends if they were okay with it.

"It's not a bad idea," Stephanie said, coming over to the counter. "Actually, I think it sounds like a lot of fun."

"But—" Tomika spluttered. "How will we ever get something together in five days' time? C.E. always takes place the night before Christmas!"

Kelsi's face cleared. "Pastor Jordan said we can choose the date we think works best since it was such short notice."

"Yeah," Cole muttered. "How about July sometime? You know, Christmas in July?"

Stephanie laughed, "Oh, Cole. It's not that bad. We'll think of something."

Aunt Sue had been listening. "You could try doing a play," she suggested. "Find a Christmas story everyone likes and act it out."

Cole thought about it for a moment. "Hey, that might work." He looked at Tomika. "Maybe Kelsi's idea wasn't so rash after all."

Tomika sighed. "I still think we should let someone else do it, but we can try."

"That's the spirit," Aunt Sue praised. "I'm anxious to see what you come up with. Why don't you get together tomorrow and discuss it?"

"I'll call everyone tonight," Kelsi promised. "C'mon, Tomika, let's go." They left in another rush of cold air.

Cole felt slightly dazed at the sudden turn of events. *Tomika's right. Someone else would be better qualified. But, I guess, we'll have to make the best of it.*

"Look at the time," Stephanie broke Cole's train of thought. "We'd better get busy if we want to be finished by five o'clock."

"Yeah, right," Cole said. "Aunt Sue was hoping to close earlier this evening. She wants to make pizza for supper."

"Lucky you," Stephanie teased. "May I join you?"

"Sure," Cole replied. "She's a great cook. In fact, she's great at everything." Cole hoped his aunt realized how much he appreciated her. He didn't know what he would do without her.

"These are the last cookies." Aunt Sue brought the tray to the table. "They should be ready to ice." She paused to survey their work. "Looks good. I'll help as soon as I've finished boxing the pies."

Finally, every cookie was adorned with a silver ball. Stephanie washed the sticky icing dishes, then left for home.

"Carry these trays to the freezer, then you may start the car and get it warmed up. I'll be out soon." Aunt Sue set the car keys on the counter. "Thanks for your help today."

"No problem," Cole said. He put the trays in the freezer, then headed out to the car. Soon, the heater was running on high. Cole turned on the music and strains of "Holy Night" filled the car.

"Nothing like Christmas music to lighten the heart." Aunt Sue smiled when she came out. "It's beautiful tonight."

It was pretty. Cole watched the big lacey snowflakes dance in the glow of the streetlamps. "Everything is so peaceful," he said, half to his aunt and half to himself. "Almost makes planning the Christmas Event bearable."

"You'll do fine," Aunt Sue encouraged. "Remember you won't be doing it alone. The rest of the youth group is involved too."

"Yeah, many hands make work light," Cole said. "That's what Grandpa would say."

Aunt Sue parked the car. "With that in mind—how about giving me a hand with the pizza preparations?"

Cole grinned. "Sure thing."

The evening passed quickly, filled with pizza and Christmas music. When everything had been cleaned up, Aunt Sue took a phone call, and Cole searched for a Christmas story in his collection of books. Aunt Sue's idea had been a good one and he figured the others would agree.

When Cole finally came across it, he knew the story was perfect. Hoping it wasn't too late, he dialed Tyrell's number.

"Hello." Tyrell sounded half asleep.

"Hey, Tyrell. It's Cole. Did Tomika tell you about the Christmas Event?"

"Yeah," Tyrell snorted. "She nearly ran me ragged—she was so worked up. So I thought I'd escape and go to bed early. Then you called."

Cole felt bad. "Sorry. I wondered if you had any ideas for the Event?"

Tyrell laughed. "I don't, but Tomika has an entire box full of Christmas stories, Christmas carol sheets—anything that has to do with Christmas. You name it—she has it."

"Great!" Cole said. "Then I'll let you get your sleep so you're able to stay awake when you give your topic at church tomorrow."

Tyrell was instantly awake. "Cole, I totally forgot about that. I'm not prepared at all—I don't even have a brief outline! You want to come over and help a friend out?"

Cole thought longingly of sleep for a moment then agreed. "Sure. I'll be over in a few minutes."

"Thanks." Tyrell cut the connection.

Grabbing his Bible, Sunday school book, and pen, Cole slipped into his denim jacket and hurried out into the night. *Can't believe Tyrell forgot about his topic. Shouldn't be too hard to dream up some Christmas theme.*

Sometimes Pastor Jordan randomly chose one of the boys to give a topic on Sunday morning. Tyrell had known about his turn for two weeks but had obviously forgotten.

Cole knocked lightly then slipped inside. Tyrell was sitting at the kitchen table poring over a concordance. Paper and books littered the table, and Tomika's box of Christmas items sat at one end. "Hard at it?" Cole asked taking the chair across from Tyrell.

Tyrell looked flustered and still half asleep. "You're a great friend, Cole. Sometime when you're in need, call me up and I'll return the favor."

"Sure thing," Cole said. "With pleasure at midnight."

Tyrell groaned, but his thoughts were elsewhere. "I hope you have some good ideas, 'cause my mind is blank tonight."

After much consideration on different Christmas themes, Tyrell decided to title his topic, "Follow the Star." Cole studied his Sunday school lesson while Tyrell scratched out an outline.

"I still don't feel prepared but at least it's something," Tyrell closed the Bible dictionary. "I'm sure glad you reminded me. I had completely forgotten."

Cole stood up. "Guess I'll head home unless you want me to stay longer." He picked up his Sunday school book and Bible with one hand and covered a yawn with the other.

"See ya," Tyrell dismissed him with a wave. "And don't let me catch you sleeping in church tomorrow." He finished with mock seriousness.

Cole grinned, "Yes, 'Dad.'"

Sunday morning, Cole slid into the pew next to Colton. "Morning," he greeted. "Poke me if I fall asleep."

Colton smiled. "Tyrell told me the same thing. What were you two doing last night?"

"Tyrell forgot he was to have a topic this morning," Cole said. "He roped me into helping him think."

The worship leader, Cole's grandpa, announced the opening song and the boys fell silent. As soon as church was over, Tomika came to where Cole was talking with Tyrell. "Kelsi said we're all invited to her house for dinner, so you better find a ride. I'm going with her family. See you then."

Tyrell's eyes lit up. "Hey, Doug just got his full license and I noticed he brought his brother's car to church this morning. He'll give us a ride since he's invited too."

Doug was more than happy to comply. "That's why I brought it," he said. "When I heard we're planning the Christmas Event today I figured the car would come in handy. Dominic was a little reluctant to hand over the keys, but I persuaded him."

They were leaving the churchyard when Cole remembered the story he had been planning on bringing. "Hey, Doug, do you mind stopping in at my house? I forgot something."

Doug didn't mind driving a little extra. "It's fun going the second mile when you've got wheels," he joked.

Tyrell gave him a playful punch. "Watch what you say. You soon won't be able to exit the car, you'll be so puffed up with pride."

"No problem of that happening," Doug shot back. "Not with so many pins in here. All I've been hearing is 'You didn't come to a complete stop,' 'Forgot to check your mirrors,' and 'Keep both hands on the wheel.' You're worse than my sister."

Cole was still laughing when he came back with his book. "This story is perfect for a Christmas play," he said, paging to the right chapter. "That is, if none of you mind acting."

"If someone minds, Tomika is bringing a whole box of other options," Tyrell put in. "I even saw a snow globe in there."

"Cole's idea is great whatever it is," Colton said quickly. "Someone else can be the snow globe."

Doug parked along the curb with some more 'helpful' suggestions from his friends. "On the way home *you* drive," he said.

Mr. Graham met them at the door. "C'mon in, young men." He smiled. "Lunch is almost ready. You'll just have to wait a few minutes while I grill the hamburgers."

The boys discussed the hockey game they had planned for Boxing Day until Kelsi announced that lunch was ready. After lunch, Kelsi told them to make themselves at home in the downstairs rec room. "I'll be down shortly. As soon as I get my younger siblings started on the dishes."

Tomika handed her box to Cole. "Take this with you. I'll see if she needs any help."

Cole looked through the box. Sure enough, there in one corner sat a snow globe. He grinned. "Last one down gets to be a snow globe in the play."

CHAPTER TWO

The rec room was neatly furnished with couches, a ping pong table, stereo system, and a few potted plants. Cole set the box on the ping-pong table and started taking the items out.

Tyrell picked up the snow globe. "Told you so." He waved it above his head. "She probably even packed those red-and-white socks I gave her last Christmas."

Tomika came down just in time to hear her brother's last sentence. "I did not."

Kelsi brought an armload of books to the table. "Did anyone else bring anything?"

"I did," Cole placed his book on the table beside Tomika's snow globe. "There's a story I thought we could rewrite as a play."

"Look at this," Tyrell said. He was still rummaging through the box. "There's a package of expired candy canes in here." He ripped the wrapper off. "Help yourselves."

Kelsi passed sheets of paper and pens out to everyone and told them to write their opinions. "Don't be shy," she added. "Every idea counts—unless it's Tyrell's."

"Hey!" Tyrell protested. "You're being partial. What's the deal?"

Cole looked sideways at him. "Maybe you should watch what you say about your sister."

"Oh," Tyrell said around his candy cane. "Yeah. Right."

Cole's pen ended up being purple. It was half dried out and wrote in an awkward, scratchy manner. Cole wrote as short sentences as possible. *Sure hope they can read this.*

Finally, all the papers were collected, and Stephanie was elected to read them. She pulled one out of the stack and glanced over it. Her brow furrowed. "Tyrell! A counting Santa's reindeer contest?"

Tyrell grinned. "Yeah. I figured since no one was going to take me seriously anyway, I may as well play the part."

Stephanie shook her head and continued reading. Aside from the reindeer contest, all the other ideas were sensible. She set the papers down and looked at Cole. "What story were you talking about?"

"Um . . ." Cole thought a moment. It was hard to concentrate with Tyrell mumbling "T'was the night before Christmas" beside him. "I thought we could act out 'The Carols of Bethlehem Centre.'" He picked up the book. "I'll have it in a moment."

Tyrell was rattling off the names of the reindeer when Doug clamped a hand over his mouth. "Give it up, Tyrell."

In the end, the final ideas were narrowed down to the Bethlehem play and a Christmas-themed mystery supper.

Tomika looked thoughtful. "We could probably do a vote," she said. "All in favor of the play raise your hands."

Cole raised his hand. As usual, Tyrell had both hands up. The vote was unanimously in favor of the play. That decided they moved into the finer details. After making a list of all the important characters, Kristy began the nominations. "All right, we need someone to be the pastor."

Doug raised his hand. "I suggest Cole," he said solemnly.

Kristy ignored Cole's protests. "All in favor of Cole being Rev. James McKenzie say 'aye.'"

Cole didn't stand a chance and Kristy wrote his name down. "Next, we need someone for Harold Thorton, the Sunday school superintendent."

"I suggest Doug." Cole grinned.

The nominations continued and Stephanie and Doug volunteered their younger siblings to be the carolers. The hour passed quickly. Finally, everyone was satisfied with the progress and Cole felt a little more hopeful about the Christmas Event. *Leave it to Aunt Sue to come up with the best ideas.*

"Enough hard work for now," Kristy set down the paper. "C'mon, Kelsi. Let's get the snack ready.

While they waited for the sisters to return, Cole hung over the arm of the couch and scanned the stack of CDs beside the stereo.

"Any new ones?" Tyrell asked lazily.

"Yeah, at least one." Cole picked up the case and handed it to his cousin. "Ever hear it?"

Tyrell shook his head. "I've heard the artist, but not this particular album."

Cole faked shock. "I thought surely the music expert would have all the latest and greatest."

"Like I said, I know the artist," Tyrell repeated. "But seriously, Cole, this album was just released this year. I'm not that desperate."

Kristy and Kelsi returned with a platter of cookies and mugs of hot chocolate. They set the snack on the table, along with a stack of red napkins. "Help yourselves," Kristy said, beckoning them to come over.

Tyrell groaned. "Why did I eat that last candy cane? Now that's what I am desperate for."

"Your hot chocolate will taste better without it," Cole replied, heading to the table for his share. "C'mon, Tyrell. You don't need everything tasting like a candy cane."

On his way back to the couch, Cole gave the snow globe a shake. While he ate a chocolate-covered ginger cookie, he watched the flakes settle on the snowman's black hat and red scarf. He couldn't' see outside, but he figured it looked much the same way. Peaceful and calm. Silent and beautiful. A comfortable feeling washed over him.

"What's up?"

Cole jumped at Tyrell's voice. "I was watching the snow globe," he said. "And thinking."

Tyrell helped himself to another cookie. "You and your thoughts," he muttered. "And I still wish I had that candy cane."

"You and your candy cane," Cole mimicked, in the same tone of voice.

Tyrell ignored him and turned to Kelsi. "We noticed you got a new CD. Like any songs on it?"

"Oh, yes. Thanks for reminding me." Kelsi picked up the case and put the CD in the player. "Any of you know 'Emmanuel'?" She selected the correct track, hit play, and the words of the song filled the room. When the last notes died away, Kelsi looked at her friends. "You like it? I though we could maybe sing it sometime."

Cole nodded. "The words are poetic. If you'd get sheet music, I'm sure we could learn it."

Tomika agreed. "While we're on the topic of music, how about singing other carols before we all leave?"

"We should sing 'Oh, Beautiful Star of Bethlehem.'" Cole didn't look at Tyrell. "Seems to me we should have sung it in church to complement a certain topic we heard."

Tyrell shoved him and nearly spilled his candy cane-free hot chocolate.

Colton grinned. "You did a good job, Tyrell, considering your hurried preparations."

"Who told you?"

Cole held a pillow over his face. "Don't ask. I'm pretending to be invisible now. You can't blame an invisible person."

"Invisible Cole," Tyrell intoned in a stern, solemn voice, "I hereby pronounce you guilty of—of—"

"Would you get to the point?" Cole peered at his cousin from behind the pillow.

Tyrell continued. "You are found guilty of telling on a friend. You owe Mr. Tyrell Woods one candy cane. Court dismissed."

Cole groaned. "Give it up, Tyrell."

Kelsi handed out carol sheets, then disappeared upstairs. Moments later, she returned. "Hey, Tyrell, catch."

Surprised, Tyrell caught the object. "Hey, thanks. A candy cane! Look at this, Cole."

In answer, Cole announced the first song. The rest of the afternoon slipped a way on strains of music. Kelsi and Kristy persuaded them to stay for a light supper and, soon after, the group prepared to leave. Colton lived nearby and decided to walk, leaving room for Doug to give Stephanie and Tomika a ride as well.

When Cole stepped outside, it was a very different world from the peaceful snow globe scene. The wind swirled the snow into a frenzy, making the town look as though it had been caught in one of Aunt Sue's vanilla milkshakes.

They piled into the car and Doug cautiously started out. Tyrell offered too much advice from the passenger seat.

Doug quickly became annoyed. "Tomika, do you have a scarf I could use to gag your brother? He doesn't know when to quit."

Tomika unwound her scarf and handed it to Cole who was sitting behind Tyrell.

Cole grinned in the darkness and silently held the scarf above Tyrell. His cousin's next "helpful" words were quickly muffled in the soft folds of cloth. "Gotcha!" Cole tied the scarf tightly to the headrest. Tyrell got the hint and wisely remained silent for the rest of the ride.

Cole had barely stepped inside the front door when the phone rang. Aunt Sue answered, then handed the receiver to Cole. "Hello." Cole leaned against the counter.

"Hi," Kelsi chirped. "Sorry to bother you, but Kristy and I were just wondering if you wanted to design the invitations for the Christmas Event?"

Cole thought a moment. "Sure thing. I'll be glad to do that."

"Thanks." Kelsi hung up.

Cole grabbed two cookies from the container, then sat down at the office computer. He stuck in his favorite CD, donned the headphones, and started designing a sample invitation.

Half an hour later, Aunt Sue touched his shoulder. Cole removed the headphones. "You wanted something?"

"Have you planned anything for tomorrow?" Aunt Sue studied the invitation. "Looks good. Are you happy with it?"

Cole saved the half-finished picture and answered her last question first. "The lettering needs improvement, but I'll work on that tomorrow. I don't have anything going."

"Then, you don't mind working extra hours?" Aunt Sue's expression was hopeful. "I want to bake cookies for the local hospital's children's ward."

"Count me in," Cole said.

The next morning, Cole dressed in his favorite yellow T-shirt, blue jeans, and an off-white pullover sweater. Aunt Sue was stirring a pot of oatmeal when he entered the kitchen.

"Good morning," she greeted pleasantly.

"'Morning," Cole replied, surprised at how cheerful she was. Normally it took his aunt a while to wake up. She wasn't the type of person who woke up just to see the sunrise.

All day, Aunt Sue hummed while she worked. Sometimes she sang.

Even Stephanie noticed. "Your aunt's in a good mood today," she said, in a low voice, when Aunt Sue left to help a customer.

"Yeah, must be the winter sunshine." Cole dropped balls of chocolate chip cookie dough onto a large baking sheet. "Not that she's normally grouchy, but she's really upbeat today."

Later that afternoon, Cole carried the garbage bags out to the dumpster. The sun hid its bright rays behind an overcast sky, and the wind's icy fingers crept behind his jacket. Another storm was approaching.

CHAPTER THREE

The day before Christmas, Cole and Aunt Sue packed the cookies in gift bags. Cole wrote *"Merry Christmas"* on slips of paper and stuck one in each bag. While Aunt Sue carried them out to the car, he ran upstairs for his wallet. *This is the perfect chance to buy Aunt Sue's gift.* He rummaged through his top dresser drawer, searching for the picture of a sweater he had clipped from a flyer. Finally he found it buried under a bunch of old tapes, some loose change, and a crumpled English assignment. Cole checked the date he had scrawled across the bottom. *Good. It's still on sale.* Aunt Sue was waiting, so he quickly stuffed the picture in his wallet and dashed downstairs. He paused at the door only long enough to step into his boots and pull his denim jacket over his white polo shirt.

On the ride to town, Aunt Sue turned down the music as if she were going to say something. Cole waited expectantly, but she turned it back up without saying a word. A minute later she did the exact same thing again.

This is strange, Cole thought. *First she literally sings every song she knows, and now she wants to tell me something but doesn't know how to say it.*

"Here we are." Aunt Sue pulled into the hospital parking lot. She led the way into the building, while Cole followed with the box full of cookie bags.

A volunteer showed them around. In one room, Cole handed a bag of cookies to a little boy with sparkling brown eyes and a bald head. Cole swallowed hard. Obviously, cancer had claimed this young child. "What's your name?" Cole tried to sound cheerful.

The boy's eyes glowed. "I'm Skyler, and I'm five years old." He held up one hand. "As old as this."

Cole grinned. "Way to go, Skyler. Soon you'll be as old as me. Guess how old I am?"

Skyler squeezed his eyes shut in concentration. Finally, he opened them and said, "Umm, twenty-five?"

"Nope." Cole hid a smile. "Ten years younger."

Quickly Skyler counted down on his fingers. "Hey, you're fifteen. That's as old as my sister."

"Right on, Buddy," Cole said. "Where'd you learn to count like that?"

The five-year-old shrugged, pleased by the praise. "In my spare time," he said. "I have lots, you know."

A lump crept into Cole's throat. "Yes, I imagine you do." He gave Skyler a smile. "Now you can eat cookies in your spare time too."

Skyler nodded. "Did you make them?"

Cole noticed a teasing glint in his eyes. Curious, he said, "I helped."

"Then I don't think they're safe to eat." Skyler had no expression on his face. "They might be dangerous."

"What's the deal?" Cole pretended to feel hurt. "I worked hard to make them for you."

"I was teasing," Skyler said quickly, afraid the older boy was seriously offended.

"You sure?" Cole wasn't about to drop his end so easily.

"One hundred percent dead certain," Skyler said solemnly.

Cole had to smile at the words. "Did you learn that in your spare time too?"

"No." Skyler seemed relieved to see the smile. "My grandpa says that. Do you know my grandpa?"

"Oh, let's see . . ." Cole thought a moment. "Is he short with white hair, a mustache, and likes to wear yellow shirts?"

Skyler giggled. "You don't know my grandpa. My grandpa is skinny," he continued. "He likes wearing *green* shirts, and he always brings me a lollipop when he comes to visit."

Aunt Sue stuck her head around the corner and motioned that she would finish handing out the cookies, so Cole could continue his conversation with Skyler. Cole handed her his remaining bags, then turned his attention back to Skyler. "Are you planning on enjoying Christmas dinner here tomorrow?" he asked.

A shadow crossed Skyler's face. "My family can't come." He fingered the edge of his blanket. "The car has a flat tire, and the tire is so patched up that Daddy isn't sure he can fix it again."

"That's too bad." Cole didn't know what to think about this sudden twist.

Skyler nodded, then brightened. "But we can still talk on the phone. Mommy calls lots every day. I think she misses me."

"Of course, she does," Cole reassured him. He couldn't imagine spending Christmas alone. *It wouldn't even seem right. I'm more blessed than I ever realized. True, I don't have my parents, but Aunt Sue has always been there for me.*

"Do you have to leave soon?" Skyler asked abruptly.

Cole glanced at his watch. "In a little while. Why?"

"'Cause I want you to read me a story." Skyler pulled a well-worn book out from beneath his pillow. "Read about Baby Jesus in the barn. He probably didn't have enough money to buy car tires either."

Cole started reading. Skyler's listened intently for the first couple of pages then his eyelid started to drift shut. By the time Cole reached the sixth page, he had fallen asleep. Easing himself off the edge of the bed, Cole silently slipped from the room and went to find Aunt Sue.

The rest of the day was spent purchasing necessities and gifts. Cole asked the clerk to wrap Aunt Sue's sweater. Then he carried it out to the car where his aunt was waiting.

"Oh, Cole. You shouldn't have!" Aunt Sue protested. "And you even paid extra to have it wrapped!"

Cole grinned. "Special people deserve to have a little money spent on them."

"Well, thanks." Aunt Sue adjusted the temperature dial. "Now that we have time to talk, what did your little friend know?"

"Skyler," Cole said, slowly. Thinking about Skyler gave him mixed feelings. He hesitated a moment and watched the brightly decorated streetlights slide by the window. "He was very disappointed that his family won't be coming tomorrow to see him. Their car has a flat tire, and they can't afford to buy a new one."

"That's terrible," Aunt Sue said.

Cole knew if he didn't let Aunt Sue in on the plan circling through his mind, she'd have the car tires bought before he could say "Merry Christmas." He hurried on. "I was thinking of having a fundraiser at the Christmas Event."

Even in the dim lighting of the car, Cole detected the pleased expression on his aunt's face. "That's a wonderful idea!" Aunt Sue exclaimed. "I'll be happy to help if you need assistance with anything."

When they reached home, Cole immediately dialed Tyrell's number. All he got was the answering machine. The recording was typical Tyrell style. Cole sighed. "Hey, Tyrell, it's Cole. Call me ASAP. I've got another idea for the Event and want to get your opinion. Thanks." He had no sooner set the phone down when it started ringing. Tyrell's number appeared. Cole answered and was surprised to hear Tomika's voice.

"Hi, Tomika. How come you got your brother's phone?"

Tomika laughed. "Oh, he doesn't know it. He had to tend the store for Grandpa, and Grandpa told him to leave his phone at home. Any surprise?"

"Not really," Cole said. "There's a pretty good chance he'd tend the phone instead of the store."

"Right on." Tomika sounded amused. "Anyway, I saw you had just tried and was too curious to wait till he calls you back. What did you want?"

Cole told her his new plan and added. "You can get a hold of the rest of the girls and see what they think."

"It's a great idea." Enthusiasm filled Tomika's voice. "I'd love to meet Skyler myself. Maybe all of us could take the money in to him after the fundraiser."

Cole agreed. "I'm sure Skyler would enjoy meeting all of you. I should let you go. Talk to you later."

He hung up and wandered into the kitchen. Aunt Sue was preparing their annual night-before-Christmas snack—popcorn and hot chocolate. "Need any help?" he asked.

Aunt Sue stirred the hot milk. "You could add butter and salt to the popcorn. Did you get a hold of Tyrell?"

"No." Cole drizzled butter over the white mountain of popcorn. "He was tending the store for Grandpa, so I talked to Tomika. She was all for it. Not that I'm surprised."

Aunt Sue smiled. "That's great. I hope everything goes well."

Cole loved Christmas Eve. There was something special about it. The smell of popcorn, the sweet taste of chocolate, and the comforting feel of friendship and love. Aunt Sue must have felt the same way because she gave Cole one of her special smiles. One that said love-you-lots-and-I-don't-know-what-I'd-do-without-you.

One of those times when it's great to be alive, Cole thought. *I wish this night would last forever.* He carried his snack into the living room and settled on the couch.

Aunt Sue handed him the Bible. "Your turn to read the Christmas story."

Cole paged to the second chapter in Luke and began reading. "And it came to pass in those days . . ." When he had finished, he sat deep in thought. *Sure would have been something to be one of those shepherds when the angels appeared. I wonder what their first thoughts were."*

Aunt Sue broke his concentration. "Cole." Her tone of voice held a hint of excitement, but yet a little hesitation.

Cole left the hills of Bethlehem and returned to the living room. "Yeah?" He swallowed the last of his drink.

"Would you like a refill?" she asked.

"Um, sure." Cole was surprised. "Is that what you wanted?"

His aunt blushed. "Actually, no." She took his mug. "I'll be right back."

Weird, Cole mused. *She's taking a long time to get that refill.* A strange sense of foreboding seemed to chase the Christmas cheer from the room.

Eventually, Aunt Sue returned. "Here you are."

"Thanks." Cole took a sip and burnt his tongue. "You were going to tell me something?"

Aunt Sue sat down, then stood up again. "Cole, I'm not sure how to say this."

Cole grinned. "I've caught on. You've wanted to tell me for awhile already, haven't you?"

"I guess I have." Aunt Sue looked a little embarrassed. "I just didn't know how to put it into words." She laughed a little. "Obviously, I still don't, at the way I'm rambling on."

"Yes, go on," Cole urged. He really wanted to know, yet somehow, he didn't.

Aunt Sue took a deep breath. "I guess I'm worried about how you'll feel about this, but—tomorrow evening I plan on having my first date."

Cole was floored. "With whom?"

"Scott Morris." Aunt Sue clasped her hands. "Remember him?"

"Yeah, somewhat. He held the revival meetings this past spring." Cole was not impressed. No one—not even a minister—could come close to being good enough for his aunt. Suddenly, Cole felt like grabbing the phone and telling Scott Morris a thing or two. This man was dealing with his aunt. Surely, Cole had some say in the matter. Inside though, he knew he didn't.

Cole's popcorn had lost its flavor. Nothing would ever taste good again. *I'll be pushed on the back burner, while Scott takes in all her smiles and love.* Cole knew he was being childish, but Aunt Sue was all he had ever known. Now she was forsaking him as well.

Aunt Sue seemed anxious for him to say something. "You don't mind, Cole, do you?"

"Yes, I do." Cole stood up. "I'm going to bed." He swallowed hard. "Good night."

"Good night, Cole," Aunt Sue said softly.

Cole scowled. *Good night, indeed. Thanks for ruining Christmas. Yeah, it'll be a great night. That's for sure.* Nothing had ever hurt so much.

The night crawled by. Cole tossed and turned till after two. He greeted the dawn of Christmas day with a headache.

"Merry Christmas," Aunt Sue said, cheerfully, when he came down.

Cole didn't see anything merry about it. Actually, it was ugly. Today, Scott Morris would be coming to see his aunt. In reply to her greeting, Cole mumbled something even he didn't understand.

The smile faded from Aunt Sue's face. She left the room and soon returned with a gift bag, which she handed to Cole.

"Thanks." Cole set it on the table and brought Aunt Sue her gift. Somehow it didn't seem like Christmas. By all appearances it was, but the essential mood was missing. Cole had a feeling it was his fault, and he felt a twinge of guilt. *Aunt Sue would be so happy, and I'm ruining it.* The thought didn't help.

Cole rummaged through the bag's contents. There was a new shirt, a gift card for a nearby bookstore, and the book *Courageous.* Cole flipped through the book and scanned the picture section in the middle. He managed to produce a smile for his aunt. "Looks interesting. Thanks a lot."

Aunt Sue put on the sweater. "It's lovely, Cole. So that's why the picture went missing from the catalogue." She gave him a teasing smile.

Cole didn't return it. He couldn't. All he could see was the face of Scott Morris, and that erased all thoughts of laughter. He carefully placed the book back in the bag and didn't look at Aunt Sue.

"We'll have to hurry if we want to get to the Christmas service on time." Aunt Sue glanced at the clock.

Methodically, Cole returned the rest of his gifts to the bag. He would have done a lot to avoid church that day. Everyone would expect him to smile, shake hands, and spread the Christmas cheer. The last thing Cole Greyson felt like saying was "Merry Christmas."

CHAPTER FOUR

Tyrell's grin was the first thing Cole saw when he stepped inside the church. That grin never ceased to amaze Cole. He didn't know anyone else who could work so much happiness into a smile.

"Good morning, Cole. And merry Christmas!"

"Merry Christmas," Cole replied weakly. "And good morning, if you say so."

Tyrell looked startled. He opened his mouth to say something, but Cole pushed past him into the auditorium. *I don't need sympathy,* Cole thought stubbornly. He slid to the far end of the bench and flipped aimlessly through a songbook. He should have known Tyrell wouldn't let it go that easily.

"What's up, Cole?" Tyrell asked in an undertone. His blue eyes were full of concern.

Cole met his gaze for a brief moment, then looked at the floor. "Don't worry about it."

"What if I want to?"

"Then—" Cole paused, searching for words. It would be a relief to share his problem with Tyrell, even if his cousin couldn't fully understand. "Then

I'll tell you, but not right now. Sometime when we're alone."

The answer satisfied Tyrell. "Okay. So how do you think our play is coming along?"

Cole shrugged. "All right, I guess. We should have something reasonable by beginning of January."

"Yeah, that's what I think." Tyrell's eyes questioned Cole's obvious lack of interest.

"Look, I don't feel like talking right now." Cole hoped he didn't sound rude. After all, it was the truth. Each tick of the clock brought Scott Morris one second closer. *How could I have been so dumb?* Cole berated himself. *I should have seen it coming. Those mysterious phone calls Aunt Sue got every once in a while. I just never expected—this, I guess.*

Aunt Sue's Christmas dinner was delicious, but Cole could hardly eat. She tried to get him engaged in conversation, but Cole refused to say more than he had to. *I don't know why she bothers when she'd rather talk to Scott,* he thought bitterly.

Eventually, Aunt Sue gave up. "If that's the way you want it—fine. Spend your entire Christmas sulking. Grow up, Cole."

Cole bit his lip and stared at his plate. His aunt rarely spoke in that tone of voice. Obviously, he had hurt her more than he thought. *But she doesn't understand,* Cole justified himself.

"I'm sorry, Cole." Aunt Sue's words were softer. "I shouldn't have said that. I'm sure this change is hard for you. Why don't you invite Tyrell over this afternoon when Scott arrives?"

Cole winced at the name. "I'd rather go over there. I wouldn't want to break up their Christmas family time."

A pained expression flitted across Aunt Sue's face. "All right. But you'll stay here till Scott arrives, won't you?"

"I can." Cole knew he had better do that much for his aunt. Much as he wanted to avoid Scott Morris, Cole knew Aunt Sue would be deeply hurt if he left before Scott arrived.

"Thanks, Cole," Aunt Sue said gratefully. "That means a lot."

Scott Morris arrived on time. Grudgingly, Cole went over and shook hands. He was taller than Cole remembered, but his voice was still as loud.

"Merry Christmas, Cole." Scott's eyes twinkled. "It's a pleasure to meet such a fine young man."

"Hi," Cole said, trying to act normal. He refused to say "Merry Christmas." He hadn't said it to his aunt, and he wouldn't say it to Scott. After all, Scott had ruined Christmas.

As soon as possible, Cole excused himself. The glaring snow hurt his eyes when he stepped outside, but the brisk wind against his face made him feel better. He managed a smile when Tomika greeted him at the door.

"Welcome, Cole," Tomika said. "I didn't expect to see you. Did your aunt kick you out of the house?" She teased.

"No." Cole forced the words to sound casual. "She's got company. I thought I'd come see Tyrell for awhile."

Tomika ushered him into the living room. "He's stuck in a book, but he'll be glad to do something else for awhile."

Tyrell's eyes lit up. "Hey, Cole."

"Hey yourself." Cole returned. Once again, Tyrell's grin had cheered him.

"Let's go to my room, and we can talk," Tyrell said. He closed his book and returned it to the shelf.

Tomika pretended to pout. "And you're going to leave me down here, wondering what you are talking about. Couldn't we play a game or something together?"

"Later, Tommy," Tyrell called over his shoulder. "C'mon, Cole."

When they reached his room, Tyrell closed the door, then sat on the edge of his bed. "All right, Cole. Spill it."

Cole leaned against the door. "You want to know what I got for Christmas?" Tyrell didn't smile. Somehow that made Cole appreciate his cousin even more.

"You know what I mean," Tyrell said. "What's bothering you?"

Cole didn't know where to begin. Finally he said, "Scott Morris." The acid in his tone surprised him.

"Scott Morris?" Tyrell repeated. "What did he do? You haven't seen him for months."

"Well, I saw him today," Cole replied evenly. "Today Scott Morris came to visit my aunt." His words dripped with bitterness.

Tyrell's mouth fell open. "You mean—you mean as a date?"

Cole nodded. "Yeah. What else? I'd have a better name for it, but that's why he came."

"Hold on a bit." Tyrell's face still held disbelief. "You should be happy, Cole."

"Well, I'm not." Cole's lip curled. "You want to know why? I'll tell you. Aunt Sue is all I have. She cared for me and loved me. Actually, she was like a mother to me. Even though my parents were taken, at least I still had her. I never knew my mom and dad, but Aunt Sue made up for them in more ways than one. At times I have wondered how life would be different if my parents were still alive, but I was happy with Aunt Sue. Until Scott Morris came along. Now, he wants to take her from me too. He's a thief! That's exactly what he is." Cole stopped his tirade to catch his breath.

The unexpected outburst left Tyrell speechless. Finally, he ventured. "Aww, Cole, I don't think so."

"Then don't," Cole said sharply. "But it's the truth." He crossed his arms and glared at Tyrell's alarm clock.

"When did you find out about this?" Tyrell asked.

Cole scowled. "Last night. She could have told me sooner, but no. She had to wait till Christmas Eve to thrust in the dagger." He fought to keep the tears from his voice.

"Hey, it's all right," Tyrell said gently. "I won't think it's strange if you want to cry."

"I *don't*." Cole raised his voice louder than he intended. "Do I look like someone who cries over every little thing?"

"Sorry I said it." Tyrell dared to meet Cole's eyes. "But if you want my opinion, it might help release some of the tension. You're pretty strung out."

"Got that right," Cole muttered. Finally he sighed and broke away from Tyrell's gaze. "Guess you probably think I was pretty immature blowing up like I did?"

"Of course not," Tyrell reassured him. "That's what friends are for."

"Well, thanks," Cole said. "I actually feel a little better. You don't mind if I stay awhile?"

"Stay as long as you like," Tyrell offered. "Do you feel up to playing a game with Tomika?"

"That would be great," Cole said quickly. "Anything to take my mind off Scott."

Tyrell grinned. "How about a game of Dutch Blitz?"

The fast-paced card game left Cole no time for extra thinking. He even felt a rush of pleasure when he managed to win the first game.

"You sure are fast," Tomika said admiringly. "You should play against Mom sometime."

"Yeah, that would be something," Tyrell agreed. "We should have a Dutch Blitz competition."

"Please, don't," Cole objected, setting out his cards for the next game. "I don't do well under pressure."

Tyrell raised an eyebrow. "You don't?" He asked, pointedly.

Cole looked down. "You know what I mean. Ready, set, GO!"

"Stop!" Tyrell protested. "I'm not ready."

Tomika grinned. "Your fault."

After many games and a lot of teasing and laughter, Tomika suggested they practice their lines for the Christmas play.

Cole put on his best preacher look and quoted solemnly, "She would be just the one if she would."

"Tomika, you don't even have any lines to practice," Tyrell said.

"I know." Tomika returned the cards to the box. "I want to hear yours."

"All right." Cole turned to Tyrell and began quoting. "Mr. Shartow, do I have your permission to put up an advertisement for the revival meetings?"

"I guess you can," Tyrell replied.

"We would be very glad, Mr. Shartow, if you would attend some of the meetings."

"It'll be a cold day when I do. The worst enemies I've got are in that church."

When the boys had finished their recital, Tomika clapped for them. "That was great! You'll do wonderful at the play."

"Yeah, especially with Cole as pastor," Tyrell grinned.

"Cut it out," Cole said, "Actually, you've got more lines to recite than I do."

"That figures." Tyrell tried to sound cross. "You always get all the breaks."

Cole thought of Scott Morris. "That's not true," he said shortly. "Whatever you do, don't envy me."

"I'm not." Tyrell hastened to explain, "I was teasing you about the story."

Cole pushed his chair away from the table. "I know, but I think I'll head home now. Thanks for everything."

Tyrell followed him to the door. "What shall I tell Tomika when she asks about you? It's pretty obvious you're upset about something."

"Say what you have to." Cole pulled on his coat. "See you at the hockey game tomorrow."

"Yeah, see you." Tyrell closed the door.

Darkness had fallen. Cole trudged on until he reached a vacant lot. There he stopped and stared up at the inky sky. "God, are You there?" He whispered the words, but they seemed to echo.

Cole wasn't expecting an answer. Of course, he knew God was there, but it would have been nice if the stars would have arranged themselves into a *"yes"* or something. He felt so alone. For a long time Cole stood there gazing at the stars. He was about to head home when a falling star streaked across the sky. Almost as fast a part of Hebrews 13:5 popped into his head.

"I will never leave thee nor forsake thee," Cole whispered. "Thank you." Somehow the loneliness waned a little. He jammed his hands into his pockets and started for the house, eager to escape the cold.

Cole pushed the door open and stood for a moment in the entrance. He could hear the rise and fall of voices in the living room. *Good. They won't see me,* Cole thought, in relief. Silently he tiptoed to his room and carefully closed the door. *They don't need to know I'm back. I don't feel like talking to anyone.* Avoiding Aunt Sue didn't make him happier but at least he didn't have to speak to anyone.

Dimly, he heard the phone ringing downstairs, then Aunt Sue's voice. "Sorry, I don't think he's here right now, but if you want to wait, I'll check." Footsteps approached the bottom of the stairs. "Cole?"

Cole scowled at his hands. "Yeah?"

Aunt Sue sounded surprised. "You *are* back. I didn't hear you come in. Anyway, Doug's on the phone."

Grudgingly, Cole took the phone and returned to his room. "Hello." *So much for that.*

"You want a ride to the rink tomorrow?" Doug asked. "Dominic's not going, but he said I can use his car."

Cole could tell Doug was impressed. "Yeah, sure that would be great. But actually now that I think of it, I might take the bus. I want to arrive alive."

"I'm rolling on the floor laughing," Doug said. "I'll come by around 9:30, if that suits."

"See you then." Cole ended the call.

Next my skates. He yanked open the closet doors. *They must be in here somewhere. Haven't used them since last winter.* A bag of books slid off the over-loaded top shelf and bounced off his shoulder, improving his temperament by negative five percent. *This closet's a mess.* Cole kicked at a box and discovered that socks offered little protection against outdated encyclopedias. He finally unearthed his skates and stick in the far corner. Cole pulled them out and brushed the dust away as best he could.

"Cole?" It was Aunt Sue again. "Would you like something to eat?"

"I'll be down," Cole called. He was starting to feel guilty about the way he was treating his aunt. *Hopefully, Scott has left already.*

When he left his room, the first thing Cole heard was Scott's deep laugh. *Sure he's happy.* Cole's fingernails dug into the palm of his hand. *Who wouldn't be happy wrecking someone else's life.* Sarcasm laced his thoughts.

"I was hoping I'd see you before I left," Scott smiled as Cole entered the dining room. "Your aunt was saying there's a hockey game tomorrow. What position do you like to play?"

"Forward," Cole mumbled. *Why does he have to be so friendly?*

Scott seemed genuinely interested in Cole's life, and Cole found it hard to give him the cold shoulder. Once he even caught himself laughing at one of Scott's jokes. Then he remembered that this man was taking Aunt Sue from him, and his smile faded. *You won't trick me into your game,* he thought scornfully.

CHAPTER FIVE

Persistent knocking awoke Cole the next morning. He rolled over groggily and tried to focus on the red numbers on his alarm clock.

"Cole?" Aunt Sue called. "Are you awake?"

The numbers finally became clear. *9:30!* Cole sprang out of bed. "Coming." He dressed frantically. Doug would arrive any minute if he hadn't come already. *How could I have slept so late?* The answer was obvious. He hadn't slept much the night after Aunt Sue had shared her "exciting" news. Cole grabbed his skate bag and headed for the stairs. He hurried, but Doug still had to wait.

"Did you sleep in?" Doug grinned as Cole shoved his skates and stick onto the floor of the backseat.

Cole climbed in after them and caught his breath. "Forgot to set the alarm. I didn't wake up till Aunt Sue called me at 9:30."

"You mean to say Christmas wore you out that much?" Colton turned in the passenger seat to face Cole.

Instead of replying, Cole changed the subject. "Are you stopping for Tyrell?"

"Nope." Doug pulled out onto the main road leading to Jefferson County. "His dad's bringing him. I guess he agreed to be one of the chaperones."

In a way, Cole was relieved. *Tyrell must think I'm the biggest fool possible.* He felt his face grow warm as memories of the night before rushed to mind. *Actually,* Cole thought, *I wouldn't mind if I didn't see Tyrell at all today.* The thought nearly made him laugh out loud. *Tyrell missing a hockey game? He'll be there, even if he has to crawl the entire way.*

Colton's question was as random as the idea of Tyrell missing the hockey game. "Have you talked to Skyler recently?"

Cole blinked in bewilderment. He'd clean forgotten about Skyler and their plans for the Christmas Event. "Uh—no. I mean, I just saw him two days ago. Guess it never crossed my mind to call and wish him a merry Christmas yesterday."

"I was just wondering since I'd never heard you mention him yet. Tyrell was the one who told me about the new plans," Colton shrugged. "Not that it really matters to me. I think it's a great idea, regardless of who tells me."

"Sorry about that," Cole said. "I guess I forgot." He noticed with relief that Doug was pulling into a parking space next to the outdoor rink.

The three boys gathered their gear and headed for the rink. Cole tied his skates in record time and moved onto the ice. The rhythm of skating felt good. He circled the rink a couple times, before heading over to where Lance Mitchell was perched on top of the side boards.

"Hey, Cole." Lance flashed his usual toothpaste-advertisement-perfect smile.

Cole hopped up next to him. "You warmed up already?"

"Yeah," Lance said. "Maybe my skills are still cold, but I'm warm." He yanked off his goalie's helmet and his ever-prominent cowlick sprang back into position.

Cole couldn't resist. "So that's how you look when you aren't behind bars."

Lance ran his fingers through his sweaty hair. "Yep. Those bars have saved my face a few times. Being goalie is dangerous work." He pointed to a small dent in the corner of the shield. "I've got Tristan to thank for that. He got a little excited and hit the goalie instead of the goal."

"You're welcome." Tristan tried to bow and do crossovers at the same time. He soon came over and joined Cole and Lance, grinning a black smile. "You ever try talkin' wish a moushguard before?" Tristan gave up and removed the guard. "Ridiculous thing. But my dad says I didn't get braces for nothing, so I wear it."

"Yeah, if we'd all play as rough as you, we'd all need mouthguards," Lance remarked. "I'd probably be wearing dentures already."

"Great joke," Tristan deadpanned.

Cole laughed. It was the natural thing to do, but it surprised him. Not much had been funny during the last day and a half. *Maybe this hockey game will do me some good,* Cole thought. *I'm becoming more cross and cantankerous as each new day dawns.* He smiled half to himself. *Must be feeling better if I'm using alliteration in my thoughts.*

"Earth to Cole. Earth to Cole," Tristan interrupted. "They're organizing teams now if you'd like to be included, or maybe the 'rinks' of Saturn are more exciting."

"That would be rings," Cole said absentmindedly. He skated after Tristan and joined the other boys clustered around Mr. Woods and Tristan's dad, Luke Smith.

"All right, fellows." Mr. Smith was a small man, but his voice made up for his stature. "A few words before we begin. Remember, we are playing to have fun—not trying to earn a place in the NHL. So be a good sport and practice Christian courtesy. For teams, why don't we start out with the ninth and tenth graders against eleven and twelve."

Everyone shifted into separate groups. Cole's team was short by one person, but that couldn't be helped as they were an odd numbered group.

"Think it'll be fair?" Tyrell asked. His expression showed no hint of thinking Cole had been foolish the day before.

"Should be," Cole said, surveying his team members. "We've got some pretty good players. Might as well give it a try."

"Okay." Tyrell turned and flashed his dad a thumbs-up.

There were more players than positions and Cole reluctantly took a place on the sidelines for the start of the game. Jackson Smith, Tristan's talkative cousin and Tony Allens, one of the twelfth graders held the face-off. *This could be interesting.* Cole suddenly didn't care that he was on the sidelines. Sometimes it was just as fun observing. Jackson was good, but then again so was Tony.

Cole held his breath as Mr. Woods dropped the puck. There was a brief struggle, then Jackson broke free and sent the puck shooting up to one of his waiting teammates. Before anyone could cheer, Tony's team had claimed ownership and was getting dangerously close to the goal. Tristan played a wonderful defense, but even so Tony scored the first goal.

During the brief interval, Tristan skated over. "Someone can take my place," he said breathlessly. "Right side defense."

Cole felt all eyes on him, so he went. He would have preferred a forward position, but defense was better than nothing.

"Let's show them," Tyrell spoke enthusiastically. He stopped the puck and flicked it on to Cole.

Cole noticed an opening near Jackson and passed the puck to the younger boy. He didn't regret it. Jackson tried for a shot at the goal, but Lance bounced the puck off his skate.

"Next time aim for the goalie," Tristan hollered to his cousin.

Cole shook his head and grinned. Sometimes he wondered if Tristan had a serious bone in his entire body. If he did, he was good at keeping it hidden.

The opposing forwards approached quickly. Cole dropped back to guard the goal and Tyrell dashed forward to meet them.

Cole didn't see it happen, but suddenly the game came to an abrupt halt. Surprised, he turned to see Tyrell skating as if in a daze to the side of the rink, his hand pressed against his chin. Cole hurried over. "What happened?" He could see blood oozing out between Tyrell's fingers.

"The puck flew up," Tyrell said barely moving his lips. His face was ashen. "How bad is it?" He slowly removed his hand and revealed the wound.

Cole winced. Mr. Woods examined it closely then put a hand on his son's shoulder. "I'm afraid you're going to need stitches, Tyrell. Your chin is split wide open."

While Mr. Woods figured out the fastest route to the hospital, Cole helped Tyrell remove his skates.

"Thanks," Tyrell said. "Play hard for me. We'll probably just head home once I'm stitched up."

Cole was about to agree when he overheard the name of the hospital Tyrell was going to. His eyes lit up. "Hey, that's where Skyler is. Maybe I should come with you."

"Fine with me," Tyrell managed a painful smile. "But I'm sure Doug would take you after the game. I don't think it's far from here."

Cole's mind was made up. "I'll let Doug know I'm going with you."

Mr. Smith had the game back in progress before they left. Cole checked the time. "The game will be over in an hour the way it is," he remarked. "I won't be missing much."

Tyrell's mind was far from the hockey game. "Get there as fast as you can, Dad," he said through clenched teeth.

"I'll do my best." Mr. Woods took the ramp and merged onto the freeway. "Thankfully, there's not too much traffic right now." He was silent for a moment then glanced at Cole. "So, who's your friend?"

Cole told him everything he knew about Skyler, and how they had met. "It'll be nice seeing him again," he finished. "He's interesting—for a five-year-old."

Mr. Woods chuckled. "Maybe I'll tag along with you and see Skyler for myself. Unless Tyrell needs me to hold his hand."

Tyrell wasn't in the mood for a quick comeback. He shook his head and his eyes said, "I don't care what you do as long as we get to the hospital."

Mr. Woods sobered. "I'm hurrying, Tyrell. I can't drive much faster, or we'll have a police escort. We'll be there in about ten minutes."

Tyrell just groaned. Cole felt sorry for him but couldn't think of anything that would get Tyrell's mind off the pain.

Mr. Woods solved that problem with five words. "I hear your aunt's dating."

"Yes," Cole said, keeping it simple. He saw Tyrell's jaw muscle twitch. *What has he all told his dad?*

Obviously not much. "I'll have stiff competition trying to keep my place as favorite uncle," Mr. Woods teased. "Scott Morris is hard to compete with."

Tyrell coughed but it came out as a strangled choke. Mr. Woods looked at him strangely. "Is something wrong?"

"My chin hurts," Tyrell mumbled, stating the obvious.

His dad didn't look convinced. "That's all? Are you sure?"

Tyrell shrugged. "I didn't really expect it to hurt that much when I coughed. That's definitely part of the reason."

Cole was relieved when his uncle didn't probe any further. *Maybe Tyrell will have more questions to answer later, but at least I won't be around.* Cole detested listening to people talk about him when he was right there.

They arrived at the hospital several minutes later. The emergency room was empty, and it didn't take Tyrell long to answer the preliminaries and get settled in a room to wait for the doctor.

Uncertain of where to find the children's ward, Cole located a map of the hospital's layout. The *"You are here"* arrow showed he was several levels beneath his desired destination. Cole turned to Mr. Woods. "Guess I'll see if I can find Skyler. You want to come along?"

Mr. Woods shook his head. "Not now. I'd better stay here in case the doctor has any questions for me. Once Tyrell's stitched up, we'll come find you and Skyler. You'll be in the children's ward?"

"Yes," Cole indicated it on the map. "See you then." He headed for the elevators and pushed the button. Eventually, one set of doors slid open. A nurse in yellow and blue tie-dyed scrubs hurried off, followed by a man who looked as if he had just stepped out of the courthouse. Every inch of his hair suit and tie was in place.

Cole automatically ran a hand over his own dark tousled hair as he entered the elevator. *Hopefully, I don't look like I came straight from a hockey match.* He pressed the three and watched the button light up.

The doors opened on the second floor. A man with a greasy ponytail and a Blue Jay ball cap worn backwards got on. "Hit the five for me, will ya?"

Cole did as he was told and felt a little better about his appearance. He watched with mild interest while the man toyed with a cigarette as if he wanted to take a drag right there in the elevator.

"Visiting family?" The man asked as the elevator lurched upward again. He pulled out a lighter then remembered where he was and stuck it back into his pocket.

"No. A friend," Cole replied. "And you?"

"That's my business," the man said huffily.

Cole felt a little miffed. *Well, sorry I was interested in your life then.* The doors opened, and Cole left with a sigh of relief. He felt the man's eyes on his back, so he turned and waved. Partially out of peaceful revenge, and partially because Cole was a peacemaker by nature.

The volunteer who had shown them around when they delivered the cookies was on duty again. "Hello, young man," she said with a smile that made her look ten years younger. "Did you bring cookies for the staff this time?"

"You're out of luck," Cole grinned. "I didn't know you were looking for any or I could have brought some."

"It's a good thing you didn't," she said firmly. "I have enough Christmas cookies to last me and mine a lifetime."

Cole laughed. "Share them with the patients."

"Good idea," the volunteer said. "So what brings you here today, if you aren't delivering cookies?"

"My cousin had an accident playing hockey. He's in the ER right now getting his chin stitched, so I thought I'd come up and visit Skyler."

The volunteer's face brightened. "Well, then. I won't keep you. Hopefully, you can cheer him. He's feeling a little blue today."

Skyler was sitting on the edge of the bed with his back to the door when Cole entered. He cleared his throat. "Hey, Skyler. What's up?"

Skyler spun around and his eyes widened. "You came back!"

CHAPTER SIX

"The Cookie Man came back," Cole grinned broadly at Skyler's look of surprise. "Did you eat all your cookies already?"

Skyler shook his head. "I have two left," he stated. "Mommy came to visit yesterday, so I gave some to her. She had to come alone, 'cause she came on the bus, but I sent some cookies back for Mindy and Adam and Daddy."

Cole did some quick calculations. Puzzled, he asked. "Did you eat any?"

"Not yet." Skyler pulled open the top drawer of the night table and grabbed the bag. "Here. You eat one, and I'll eat one."

"No sir, buddy." Cole refused the offered cookie. "They're all yours. I have more than enough at home."

"Okay." Skyler didn't argue. He returned the bag to the drawer, then asked, "Did you hurt yourself?"

"Hurt myself?" Cole repeated. "Why do you ask that?"

"Because you're here." Skyler threw his arms wide to include the entire hospital. "Or maybe you brought more cookies?"

"No cookies." Cole understood now. "I came with my Uncle Philip and my cousin Tyrell. Tyrell was playing hockey, and the puck his chin and split it open."

Skyler's eyes grew large. "Is he all right?"

"Yeah," Cole said. "He's getting stitches right now, and then he's coming to see you."

"Really?" Excitement filled Skyler's face. "This is the best day ever!"

"Yes," Cole said, "for me too. Do you know why?"

Skyler shook his head. "Why?"

"Because today I got to visit you!" Cole grinned as Skyler ducked his head shyly. "Why don't we talk while we wait for Tyrell.

Skyler was a great conversationalist, and by the time Tyrell and his dad arrived, they had discussed many different topics.

"Wow. Are you really a hockey player?" Skyler asked, the minute Tyrell stepped inside the door.

"An unprofessional sorry-looking one," Tyrell said, carefully. "So, you are Skyler."

Skyler beamed. "Yes," he answered, then asked, "Does your cookie friend play hockey?"

Tyrell raised an eyebrow. "My cookie friend? Oh, if you mean Cole, then yes."

"Yeah, whatever his name is." Skyler looked at Cole.

"That's me," Cole said. "I guess I never told you my name. Sorry about that."

"Don't worry," Skyler replied quickly. "I just called you my cookie friend. He turned his admiring gaze on Tyrell again. "Did it hurt a lot?"

So, Tyrell related the whole story to the ears of his eager young listener. "And now I have seven stitches as a reward."

Cole looked at him and shook his head in amusement. "Did they try mummifying you in the process as well?" He grinned, indicating the white gauze wrapped around Tyrell's head.

Tyrell grimaced. "I remove that in twenty-four hours, and if I get my way, it'll be twenty-three."

"Twenty-four, young man," Mr. Woods remarked, mildly.

"May I have your autograph?" Skyler asked brightly. He pulled a stub of a pencil out of his pocket and fished around in his drawer until he found a scrap of paper.

"I'd be honored." Tyrell took the paper and scribbled his name with a flourish. "You know, you're my first fan, Skyler."

Skyler was impressed. "Someday I want to see you play."

"You do that." Tyrell grinned.

Mr. Woods interrupted their conversation. "I don't want to rush off, but we should keep going. It was nice meeting you, Skyler. Hopefully, we can drop in again sometime soon."

"Wait, Dad," Tyrell said as his dad turned to leave. "I know I look rather rough, but could you take a couple pictures of us three?"

Cole agreed. "Great thinking. We'll get one developed and framed for you, Skyler."

Skyler's smile was enormous as Cole and Tyrell pressed in on either side for the picture. It got even bigger when Mr. Woods showed him the digital image. "I love it," he breathed, sounding much older than his five years.

The trio left after promising someone would return with a framed copy. "I can see the photo caption already," Cole said mischievously. *"Skyler, Cole, and Wounded Hockey Player."*

Tyrell studied the picture. "Yeah, but at least my face isn't swollen too badly."

"Not yet, anyway," Cole replied. He yanked open the truck door and hopped inside.

As Mr. Woods turned the truck in the direction of Appleton, Tyrell grimaced at his reflection in the mirror. "It's starting to swell more already. Dad, did you tell Mom what happened?"

"I thought I'd let you," Mr. Woods said. "You could call now in case they're wondering where we are."

"Okay." Tyrell pulled out his phone.

Cole watched his cousin. By Tyrell's misshapen grin, he had a feeling Tyrell wasn't going to let on what had taken place. He wasn't disappointed.

"Hey, Tommy," Tyrell drawled. "You wondering where we are? Oh . . . We'll be home in about twenty minutes . . . Yeah . . . Oh, and just so you know, I'm bringing a surprise home . . . No, I can't give you a hint . . . Sorry, you'll have to wait . . . Yeah, see you then. Bye."

Cole snickered. "You're mean, Tyrell. Now she thinks you're bringing her a gift."

"I want to see their reaction," Tyrell said with satisfaction. "I can picture Tomika already. Her mouth will drop open, and she'll gasp in a horrified tone, 'Tyrell, whatever happened?' Mom will come running when she hears Tomika and turn pale. It will be well worth it."

"Yeah, I imagine it will be," Cole sighed. He wondered what Aunt Sue would say if he came home with stitches. Before Scott Morris had appeared on the scene, Cole knew his aunt would have worried over him until he was embarrassed. But would she do that now, or would she say *Cole, you should have been more careful. Now you'll look like you were in a fight when Scott comes next week.* After all, Scott was more important than an orphaned nephew. Cole shifted uncomfortably and was suddenly glad he didn't have to find out.

Obviously, Mr. Woods was thinking of Scott Morris as well. "So, Cole, did you and Scott have a chance to talk?"

"Yeah," Cole hoped he didn't sound unwilling. "We talked about hockey and stuff like that."

Mr. Woods nodded, then teasingly asked the question Cole had been praying he wouldn't. "What's your opinion? Is he good enough for your aunt, or are you ready to ship him out?"

Making a mental note never to ask anyone that question, Cole shrugged. "It's not my decision."

"Hey, Dad." Tyrell's words sounded funny. Partly because his lips were swollen and partly because — Cole thought he knew why. Tyrell continued. "Did you see that sign? I didn't know there was a Chevy dealer this close to home. Must have just moved in. Why don't you trade the truck in and get a new one?"

Cole was as startled as Mr. Woods.

"Tyrell, I only bought this one last year. It's in perfectly good condition. We can put our money to better use than buying a new truck every year."

"Yes, Dad," Tyrell said.

Cole stared hard at the back of his cousin's head. *Oh boy, Tyrell. Is your dad ever going to wonder what's up?!*

Mr. Woods pulled up in front of the house. Cole pushed the door open. "Thanks for the ride," he said, grabbing his stick and skates. He breathed a sigh of relief, grateful to escape the confining questions.

Tyrell fumbled with the door handle then followed him. In a low voice, meant only for Cole's ears, he said, "Sorry about that. I didn't know he'd ask about . . . well, everything."

Cole smiled faintly. "He's going to be asking you about everything."

"Yeah." Tyrell didn't look concerned. "Maybe, but that's not the first time I've acted weird."

"It's not your fault," Cole protested. "Don't worry. I've learned my lesson. Never put up a false front just to look good. If I had told your dad how things stood right from the beginning, you wouldn't have had to try changing the subject to cover for me. This will go down in my diary for sure."

Tyrell's eyebrows rose. "You keep a diary?"

"Sort of and not really," Cole said. Sometimes he enjoyed saying things that made no sense. "Actually, all it is is a stack of sticky notes. Every evening before bed, I pull one off and say 'Cole, what did you learn today?' then I write it down, fold it up, and throw it in a box. Maybe someday I'll go through it."

"Interesting." Tyrell laughed as well as he could through swollen lips. "Anyway, I'm holding Dad up. Doug mentioned something about a Christmas play practice tomorrow, so maybe I'll see you then."

Cole waved and headed for the house. He found Aunt Sue in the kitchen baking a variety of desserts she never made at the bakeshop. Cole pushed up his sleeves and decided to be reasonable. "You want any help?"

Aunt Sue spun around at the sound of his voice, nearly knocking a carton of eggs off the counter. "You're back. I was getting worried."

"It got a little late," Cole admitted. Her smile made him feel guilty about his earlier thoughts, and he proceeded to tell the whole story.

"That's awful." Aunt Sue's voice filled with sympathy. "But I'm also glad you had a chance to see Skyler again. I'm sure that made his day."

Cole remembered Skyler's ear-to-ear grin and nodded. "Yeah, he was enthralled with Tyrell. Guess he thinks the only hockey players worth noticing are the ones who get hurt."

Aunt Sue laughed and handed him a green mixing bowl. "You can stir this together and make muffins to put in the freezer for Sunday mornings."

Cole stirred vigorously, and the flour flew, creating a miniature snowstorm in the kitchen. "Guess that was a little rough," he said, surveying the mess.

"Remember, the hockey game is over." Aunt Sue smiled. She handed him a measuring cup half full of flour. "Add this and you should be okay."

When the batter reached the right consistency, Cole added blueberries and scooped the dough into muffin tins. It was a somewhat messy job, but then again, he preferred that over something painstakingly neat—like putting silver balls on top of Christmas tree cookies.

"Mind if I turn on the music?" Aunt Sue asked.

"Nope." Cole had been waiting for the question. He got his love for music honestly enough. Its heart had throbbed steadily through the generations before him, and he wasn't about to let it stop at him.

The first song was a well-worn Christmas chorus and not necessarily Cole's first choice. He transported himself back to Thanksgiving as the singer tried wishing him a merry Christmas. The next song, however, jolted him away from turkey and cranberry sauce. It defied any Christmas categories. Aunt Sue handed him a sandwich and a glass of milk, along with an explanation.

"I felt like listening to some non-Christmas songs today, so I put a couple of CDs on random."

Cole rather liked random. It was, well . . . random. He chewed his sandwich to the beat of "Sound the Battle Cry" and tried to guess what the next song would be.

The phone rang and Aunt Sue turned the music down. Cole knew by her smile that the caller could be none other than Scott Morris. He focused on the song until he heard her say, "Sure he's available. Just a second."

Barely conscious of what he was doing, Cole headed for the front door. He paused only long enough to grab his hooded jacket. "I'll be gone for a bit—don't keep supper waiting just for me."

Tyrell did a poor job of concealing his surprise when Cole knocked. "You again?"

Cole decided not to take offense and to say things as they were. "Yeah, I had to get out of the house."

"Had to?" Tyrell frowned. "Your aunt wanted you to clean your room or something?"

"Or something." Cole agreed. "Scott called and wanted to *talk* to me."

Tyrell whistled. "Hey, neat. What did he want?"

"I don't know," Cole sighed. "That's why I left."

"Oh."

For the first time Cole keenly felt his cousin's disapproval. "You don't think that was the right thing to do, do you?"

Tyrell didn't say anything for a moment. When he did speak, he didn't look at Cole. "Well, personally, I think you were kind of rude."

"Rude?!" Cole always admired Tyrell's open honesty, but this time it hit a little too close to home. "How can you say that?"

"Because I'm your cousin," Tyrell replied. "And because I think you'd be better off facing your problems instead of running from them. Do you think it'll be any easier talking to Scott at a later date?"

Cole had to admit Tyrell had a pretty good point. "Not exactly, but . . . ."

"But what?" Tyrell asked forcefully. "You planning on running until you can't anymore?"

"No, I just . . . think it might be easier," Cole finished lamely. He could tell by the look on Tyrell's face he had said the wrong thing.

"Definitely not," Tyrell said firmly. "And trust me. It just makes everything worse. I've tried it before."

CHAPTER SEVEN

"True," Cole said. "It's also true you haven't been in my shoes." Immediately, he wished he could take the words back.

Tyrell's eyes filled with hurt. "Hey, don't come to me then. I just told you my opinion. That's all."

"Sorry," Cole relented. "Let's change the subject. How are you feeling?" He indicated the white bandage.

"Oh, all right considering." Tyrell obviously didn't want to drop the first topic. "Cole, have you talked to anyone else, other than me, about this?"

Cole blinked. "No." After a moment he added, "I don't want to either."

"Which could be another problem," Tyrell said. "Talk to some adult you trust—Grandpa, my dad, or maybe, most importantly, your aunt."

"No!" Cole said, emphatically. "I mean, not now, not yet."

Tyrell looked disappointed. "Okay. Whatever. I can't make you. It's your decision. I was just voicing my opinion as usual. And, as usual, no one wants to hear it. Just ask Tomika."

"She's no better." Cole forced a grin. He didn't feel like talking anymore. "Guess I'll head home," he said, wanting to do that even less.

Aunt Sue was waiting for him when he returned. She didn't say much though—just handed Cole the phone and a scrap of paper with Scott's number on it. "He's waiting for you to call him back."

Cole knew better than to argue. One look at Aunt Sue's face would have told anyone the same thing. Without a word, he headed to his room. Cole sat on the edge of his bed and stared at the phone. The phone gazed blankly back. Unlike Tyrell, it didn't offer any opinions. He almost wished it would. He crumpled the paper scrap into a tiny ball, then slowly uncrumpled it. He hadn't dreaded anything so much since the time he had accidently pitched a baseball through Mrs. Rushmore's car window and had to go find her.

"Brace up, Cole," he told himself sternly. "You dug the hole for yourself, so it's up to you to get yourself out of it." After mentally scolding himself for five more minutes, Cole gathered up enough courage to dial the number. He listened to it ring and hoped he'd reach the answering machine.

"Hello, Scott Morris speaking," said a clear voice.

Making a mental note of Scott's politeness, Cole explained who was calling.

He could hear the smile in Scott's voice. "So you're back from your fast trip?"

"Yeah," Cole said weakly. *What did Scott want anyway?*

"I'll make this quick since you probably have other things to do. (Cole didn't, but he wasn't about to say otherwise.) I was wondering if you wanted to go ice fishing with me sometime next week?"

Cole's jaw dropped. The idea was nearly unthinkable—spending the day fishing with Scott of all people. But he couldn't turn down the offer, so he said, "Do you mind if I bring my cousin along?" Tyrell would make things more bearable.

Obviously, Scott's thoughts didn't fall into the same category. "Sorry, Cole. I was hoping just you and I could go. Will it suit for Tuesday? I'm off work, and you won't be back in school yet."

Cole tried in vain to think of an excuse. Finally, he said, "Yeah, I guess that should work. See you then."

After he hung up, Cole once again stared at the phone. *Scott wants to take me ice fishing!* Cole had never gone ice fishing before. It was something on his bucket list. *I just didn't plan on doing it with Scott.*

Wanting to avoid telling Aunt Sue about their conversation as long as possible, Cole sprawled across the bed and recited the play lines to himself. Since everything was going well, and they had managed to shorten the play to under fifteen minutes, the Christmas Event was scheduled for Tuesday night. Tuesday night! Cole shot straight up. *There's my excuse for Scott.* He thought a moment longer. *Problem is, I'm not so desperate that I want to call him back. Besides, I sort of want to go fishing. I guess I'll just tell him I have to back by four in the afternoon.* Immediately, the Tuesday fishing trip appeared more bearable.

Cole returned to the kitchen, avoided Aunt Sue's curious eyes for ten minutes, then finally told her about the phone call. "I'll have to be back by four to help set up for the Christmas Event though," he finished.

Aunt Sue nodded. "I'm sure Scott will understand. Even so, it sounds like you'll have fun."

"Yeah, I guess so," Cole said grudgingly. *Why is it so hard to admit liking Scott?* He had to agree that Scott would be a great uncle, but inside something held him back from expressing it. Something he couldn't quite explain or maybe didn't want to.

* * *

The Saturday night rehearsal went surprisingly well. They invited Pastor Jordan and his wife to be the audience, and they gladly complied.

The performance of his friends' younger siblings amazed Cole. Obviously, they had practiced a lot at home. Cole turned to Tyrell. "They're singing those songs by memory, aren't they?" He couldn't see anything from where he and Tyrell waited off stage.

"I think so," Tyrell said.

The singing stopped, and Cole took a deep breath. He heard Colton pull the curtain shut and knew it was his cue to get on stage and help set up the props for the final act. It was also the part where Cole had the stage all to himself for the first bit.

Everything was put in place, and Cole sat down at the makeshift desk. The chair felt a bit unsteady, but then again, a studying preacher wasn't supposed to be fidgeting.

The curtains were pulled back. Cole tried to study and not glance at the audience, which had grown to include the young singers and all the other actors, with the exception of Tyrell, Kelsi, Kristy, and himself.

The door in the wall set up almost in the middle of the stage vibrated with knocking. Cole stood up and went to answer it. *I'll have to remember to tell Tyrell to calm down on the knocking.*

Cole opened the door before Tyrell knocked the wall over. "Good evening, Mr. Shartow. Won't you come in?"

Tyrell started to say, "I've come for help," when a childish voice belonging to Doug's brother Chase, said in a stage whisper, "Hey, Seth! Tyrell looks like he fell in a blueberry pie."

Instinctively Tyrell's hand went to his chin and everyone's eyes followed. Cole snickered a very "un-preacherish" snicker. Tyrell grimaced, and the audience tried not to laugh.

As soon as the play ended and the curtains had closed, Doug raced on stage very apologetic. "I'm sorry! I thought Chase knew better than to say things like that aloud. Although," he peered closely at Tyrell's face, "that was a pretty good description. Did you get a little greedy or did you forget where your mouth was?"

"You're a good friend but a poor guesser," Tyrell said. "You also have a horrible memory. No offense meant, of course."

"Of course," Doug mimicked.

Cole broke into the conversation before a friendly argument could start. "Did you get the picture developed yet?"

Tyrell nodded. "Yeah, but I left it at home. Skyler's one hand is a little blurry but otherwise it's okay. Tomika was so impressed she wanted to blow it up and put it on canvas. She said I looked *cute* all wrapped up like a Christmas gift." Tyrell made a face.

Doug chuckled. "I want to see this picture."

"We'll be setting it by the fundraiser box Tuesday night," Cole said. "And, by the way, Tyrell, calm the knocking down a little. The wall wobbled when I went to open the door."

"Yeah, I caught on." Tyrell looked a little sheepish. "Don't worry. I'll calm it down. Wouldn't want to squash the preacher."

"Thanks, Mr. Shartow," Cole returned. "Your consideration is greatly appreciated."

Tomika hurried by with a glue bottle and started gluing a rung back onto the leg of Cole's wobbly chair.

"Hey, thanks a lot," Cole said. "How'd you know something was wrong with it?"

Doug answered for her. "Easy. You looked exactly like someone who was sitting on a chair with something wrong with it."

"Very funny," Cole grinned. He headed toward the back of the stage where the other things were pushed into a corner. "Let's check the other props and stage paraphernalia and make sure all is in order."

They did a quick but thorough examination. Everything appeared to be in good condition, though Tyrell wasn't sure about the chair Tomika had fixed. He wiggled the rung with a thoughtful frown. "Seems a little loose."

Cole groaned. "Give the glue a chance to dry. Admit it, Tyrell. She did a fine job even though she's your sister."

"Yeah, yeah," Tyrell grumbled good-naturedly. "Surprise, surprise."

"Well, you can spend the evening fussing over the chair," Cole told him. "See you around." He left the stage and started for the back of the auditorium, where Pastor Jordan was holding a lively conversation with the young singers, Seth, Kai, Chase, and Lynn.

"Good evening, Pastor," Cole said, during a lull. "Glad you could come."

"Thanks for the invitation." Pastor Jordan excused himself from the circle and turned to face Cole. "That's an excellent play you have going there. Colton told me it was your idea."

"Not exactly," Cole said. "Sure, I chose the story, but it was Aunt Sue's idea for a play. We're also doing a baked goods fundraiser."

"Do you have a date in mind for this to take place?"

Cole nodded. "That's what I wanted to talk to you about. We were wondering if you'd mind announcing it tomorrow. We plan on Tuesday night at 7:00 here in the church basement."

"Sounds good," Pastor Jordan replied. "I'll be looking forward to the final event. Oh, and by the way, tell your aunt congratulations. I'm sure excitement levels are high around your place." He studied Cole's face closely.

"Definitely for Aunt Sue," Cole stated shortly.

Pastor Jordan's expression never changed. "I see," he said and turned to leave. He stopped abruptly and placed a hand on Cole's shoulder. "Remember, son, I'm praying for you. Not all change is easy. Trust God, leave it in His hands, and things will turn out for the best." Then he was gone.

Cole stared at the floor without seeing it, until he became aware that the younger boys were crowed around him, vying for his attention.

"Hey, Cole. I have a joke for you," Chase said with an exact replica of his older brother's grin. "Doug told it to me. Knock, knock."

Cole swallowed hard and managed a weak response. "Who's there?'

"Choo."

"Choo who."

"Did you hear the train?" Chase burst out laughing and so did his friends. "Now it's your turn, Cole."

Seth studied Cole solemnly for a moment. "I don't think he can tell jokes tonight. He looks sad."

For some reason, Seth's statement made Cole laugh. "Actually, I do have one for you. Who went into the lion's den and came out alive?"

Kai looked at him reproachfully. "Daniel. But that's not even a joke. You must be really sad."

"Wait. I'm not finished yet," Cole hurried on. "Who went into the tiger's den and came out alive?"

Lynn started to say "Daniel," but the other three boys shook their heads. "He said, 'tiger's den.'" Chase corrected importantly.

Cole was hearing some pretty absurd guesses when Tyrell sauntered over. Immediately, Seth pounced on him. "Who went into the tiger's den and came out alive?"

"Without thinking, Tyrell said, 'Daniel.'"

"Tricked you," Seth cried gleefully. Then he frowned. "But I don't know the answer either."

"Think about it," Cole replied. "If you still haven't found the answer by tomorrow, I'll tell you." He glanced at his watch. "Guess I'll head home. I'm sure Tyrell would like to hear some jokes. Good night, everyone."

No one replied, and poor Tyrell was bombarded with jokes. Cole grinned and left. The night air sparkled with a few snowflakes, drifting through the icy stillness. Cole paused on the sidewalk and watched his breath float away in frosty clouds. Just as he began tracing his footsteps home, Tyrell raced after him. "Hey, Cole! Wait up!"

Cole stopped and waited for his breathless, coatless cousin to catch up.

"Glad I caught you in time," Tyrell puffed. "Dad wanted me to deliver this." He pulled a small envelope from his pocket. "Here."

"Uh, thanks." Cole took the envelope. His name was written across the front in his uncle's trademark scrawl. He glanced at Tyrell, but his cousin's expression revealed nothing of the envelope's contents.

Tyrell started back toward the church, rubbing his bare arms. "See ya. I'd talk longer, but I'm a little cold."

* * *

The envelope contained a card. Cole traced the red and black diamond design several minutes before reading his uncle's note. He had a feeling he knew what it was about. Finally, Cole took a deep breath and began reading.

My dear nephew Cole,

"Casting all your care upon Him for He careth for you." (1 Peter 5:7) First of all, I want to apologize. I did not realize how you felt about the situation and am sorry for saying things that may have hurt you. It was not my intention, and I hope you'll forgive me. Just a word of advice—please find someone you feel comfortable with and tell them how you feel.

God bless, your Uncle Philip

For the second time that night, Cole blinked back tears.

CHAPTER EIGHT

Apparently appointed spokesman, Chase approached Cole the minute church let out. "We gave up," he said. "What's the answer?"

Cole grinned. "The tiger."

"Oh." Chase's eyes widened, then he giggled. "That's funny. Of course, it was the tiger."

"Now you have a riddle for Doug," Cole replied. "See how smart he is." He smiled at Chase's enthusiastic nod. Taking a number of Christmas Event invitations, Cole went to talk with Mr. Barkley, his grandpa. "Do you mind setting these out at the store?"

"I'd be glad to." Grandpa took the invitations. "Do you have any plans for this week before school starts?"

"Yeah, Scott wants to take me ice fishing on Tuesday, and I figure we'll deliver the money we get at the fundraiser to Skyler's family sometime as well."

"So, your ice fishing wish is being fulfilled." Grandpa looked pleased. "I'd have enjoyed taking you, but it seems the store business is keeping me too busy."

Cole reassured him. "Don't feel bad about it." He hesitated a moment. "Anyway, I think maybe Scott and I need this opportunity to get to know each other." He was surprised at how hard it was to say the words aloud.

* * *

The truck tires hummed steadily on the pavement. Cole stared straight ahead, well aware of the driver's presence. *I will have fun today,* Cole told himself for the seventh time that morning. *If Scott plans on being my uncle I need to accept it.* He'd been thinking along that line ever since he'd read Mr. Woods' apology. *If I accept the idea, I won't have to tell anyone about my struggle to like Scott. Obviously, Uncle Philip and Tyrell think I should, but I don't want to.* Deep inside, Cole felt that acceptance would be hard to attain.

Scott stopped whistling "Hark! The Herald Angels Sing" and spoke to his silent passenger. "So, do you enjoy ice fishing?" He chuckled. "Maybe that's a poor question, since we're on our way all ready."

Hating the feeling of resentment that rose in him at the sound of Scott's voice, Cole tried to quench it. So much for acceptance. "Actually, I've never gone before, but I do enjoy fishing."

"Then you should have fun today." Scott fell silent and soon resumed his whistling. Half an hour later he turned onto a sideroad. "We'll arrive at the lake in about ten minutes. You said you have to be home by four?"

Cole nodded. "I should be. Are you planning on being at the play tonight?"

"I sure am," Scott said. "Sue invited me since I'm in the area anyway."

"I figured." Cole looked away. Tonight everyone would see Scott and Aunt Sue together. *And tonight,* Cole thought, *I plan to avoid them.* Immediately all his intentions of acceptance came flooding back. *This is going to be harder than I'd counted on.*

Scott parked the truck near the lakeshore. "The lake froze over early this year, but I still wouldn't feel safe taking the truck out. I hope you don't mind walking. We'll stay fairly close to shore though since we have to leave in three hours.

Shouldering the ice auger and carrying a small propane stove, Scott started out. Cole followed with the remaining two sacks which contained the fishing equipment, bait, and lunch. The farther from shore they walked, the windier it became. Cole zipped his coat up farther and was glad the temperature had risen since the night before.

Finally, Scott reached the desired destination. "There's usually pretty good action here," he said.

To Cole, that section of the lake looked like any other. Windswept snow swirled around his boots and was lost in a vast whiteness. Cole set the bags down next to the propane stove.

Scott started the ice auger and set to work drilling holes. Cole watched with interest. The process of ice fishing was entirely new to him, and he meant to learn as much as possible. Scott drilled five holes then set the auger aside.

Cole was puzzled. "Are you expecting more people to show up, or why so many holes?"

Scott laughed. "I'll get you set up at one hole and I'll tend the other four."

"Wow." For the first time that day, Cole felt no resentment. "You are a serious fisherman."

"You bet I am." Scott grinned boyishly. "When I was younger, I spent every spare moment with my fishpole. I grew up near a lake and considered myself the luckiest boy around. My sisters could never understand what was so great about fishing but every now and again I'd convince someone to join me."

"So, you don't like fishing alone?" Cole asked taking the short pole Scott offered him.

"Nope." Scott winked. "No competition. Only bright thing about fishing alone is you always catch the biggest fish."

Cole baited his hook following Scott's example, then waited further instructions.

"All right. You can fish there." Scott pointed to the nearest hole. "Just let out line till it reaches the lake bottom then reel in about an inch or so. After that, all you need to do is jig the bait, and hook any fish that comes along. Oh, and send all the big ones to my hole." He winked again.

Cole grinned. "Yeah right. And what if I don't?"

"Don't get smart with me," Scott teased, trying to sound stern. "Nothing's stopping me from making you wait in the truck till it's time to leave."

"Yessir." Cole laughed. Scott could be a lot of fun, and for some reason Cole was starting to feel like a yo-yo. Up one moment, down the next. Half of his heart said he should accept Scott and the other half held back. If Cole was completely honest with himself, the constant up and down motion was wearing him out. He had a lurking feeling that sooner or later he would reach the end of the string. It wasn't a pleasant thought, and Cole hoped the fish would start biting.

Scott broke his train of thought with a yell, and Cole turned to see his might-be uncle dashing through the snow toward the farthest hole. Once he nearly fell but managed to keep his balance. Cole could see the pole bobbing up and down and found Scott's excitement catching. He strained to see better. Suddenly there was a jerk on his own line.

"I got a bite!" He hollered to Scott, unsure if he were to handle it like any other.

With a triumphant shout, Scott landed his fish then turned to Cole. "Set the hook! Start reeling in!" He started running to Cole's aid.

Cole had never in his life seen anyone get so excited over a fish. He broke out laughing, and nearly lost the fish in trying to regain his composure before Scott reached his side.

"Nice fish," Scott said admiringly as the fish flopped on the snow. He measured quickly. "Eighteen-and-one-half inches. Hey, it's bigger than mine."

"Maybe it didn't get your message in time," Cole said, feeling mischievous. "Better luck next time."

But Scott was already streaking toward the next bobbing line. Cole watched in amusement as Scott slipped on a patch of bare ice. He tried crawling the remaining three feet, but his knees just spun on the slick surface. When he finally reached the hole, the fish was gone.

Cole felt weak with mirth. Watching Scott fish was as good as fishing in itself. He definitely hadn't counted on the extra entertainment, but he wasn't about to complain.

Scott came back grumbling good-naturedly about his bad luck and bruised knees. "Go ahead and laugh," he told Cole. "Once you've had more ice fishing experience, I'll set *you* up with four holes, and then it will be *my* turn to laugh."

The smile faded on Cole's face. *Scott really plans on sticking around, doesn't he. What if I don't want him to? Don't my votes count?* Immediately contrary thoughts followed. *I wouldn't mind Scott for an uncle. Maybe God is sending him to take the place of my dad.* Cole liked the thought. In fact, he really, really liked it. No sooner had it crossed his mind when he got a sick feeling in his stomach. *What if they do get married, and Scott decides he doesn't want me living with them.* The possibility was too awful to even spend time dwelling on. Cole started jigging as though his life depended on it, hoping to push away the thought. Suddenly, he became aware that Scott was still standing near his ice hole. Startled, Cole looked up and met Scott's eyes.

"Are you all right?" Scott's voice held concern. "I thought you knew I was teasing—about laughing at you fishing with four holes."

"It's not that," Cole said with an edge to his voice.

Scott still looked puzzled. "Do you care to tell me?"

The thought of possible rejection made Cole too upset to reason. He turned to Scott, fire in his eyes. "All right, I'll tell you." Cole tried to keep his voice calm and controlled. "The problem is you!"

"Oh." Scott's eyes never left Cole's. "Do you want to talk about it?"

"No," Cole said, but as soon as the word left his mouth, he did. He broke Scott's gaze and concentrated on the fishing pole.

Instead of pressing further, Scott changed the subject. "I'll make lunch now. Yell if there's any action."

Cole gave a slight nod. An audible answer might have betrayed the emotion he felt. Out of the corner of his eye, he watched Scott go about lunch preparations. The tiny propane stove was put to use and, in a short while, the wieners were sizzling. Scott wrapped them in tinfoil and poured a can of beans into the frying pan.

"Hey, Cole. C'mon over and help yourself," Scott called. "I made lots."

The food tasted delicious, but Cole had to force himself to choke down a sizeable portion. Embarrassment had a cruel way of chasing away hunger. So did worry. So did the fact that Scott kept throwing him concerned glances.

Long before the last hour had ticked past, Cole was wishing he were anywhere but where he was. The ice fishing trip lay shattered like the shards of a broken dream.

"Cole." Scott called for his attention. "Are you ready to leave?"

"I sure am." Cole realized how happy he sounded and added, "My feet are getting cold."

"Yeah, that tends to be the age-old ice fishing complaint. I'll have to take you boot shopping." Scott grinned.

"Yeah, maybe," Cole mumbled. *Yeah, right. Boot shopping. Who does Scott think he is anyway?"*

In silence, he followed Scott off the lake to the truck. They drove for ten minutes before the muteness was broken. "I'd say we did pretty good today," Scott began. "Even though we could only keep the first two—and yours was bigger than mine."

Cole stiffened and made himself nod. He knew by Scott's voice that the man wanted to take the conversation much further.

Scott thoughtfully tapped his fingers against the steering wheel and cleared his throat. "Cole, I want you to tell me how I am the problem. I can't change anything if I don't know what I'm doing wrong."

"Forget it," Cole said. Scott's good attitude shamed him, and suddenly he saw things with more clarity than before. His answer didn't satisfy Scott.

"Why should I?" Scott's voice was kind. "Cole, maybe you haven't caught on, but I care about you. I don't want you to spend your entire life in misery just because I'm doing something that hurts you."

Funny, you should say that. How about forgetting you ever knew my aunt. Cole's thoughts were sarcastic, but aloud he said nothing.

Scott continued. "I want you to tell me. Life will go better for both of us if you say what's on your mind."

There it was again. The same old repetitive theme. The wording changed some, depending on the speaker, but the message could be melted down to one word—*talk.* That formed the problem. Cole did not want to talk. At least not to Scott. Deep inside he knew he wanted to talk to someone, wanted to pour everything out to them, but no one seemed right. So Cole waited.

Scott was waiting as well. "Please, Cole." He didn't demand, but his tone implored an answer.

Cole relented a little. "Forget it," he repeated. "I'm beginning to think the real problem is myself." He could see Scott did not approve of the answer.

"Okay," Scott said slowly. "If you are absolutely sure."

"I am."

Scott frowned. "But are you?" He asked quietly, more to himself than to Cole.

Immediately, Cole turned his attention to the passing scenery. He tried to ignore the fact that Scott's thoughts were probably on him. The tapping fingers indicated as much.

By the time they had reached the outskirts of Appleton, Cole had had enough of Scott's tapping. He was also tired of feeling sorry for himself. *You'd think I'd know better by now, Cole* thought. *I must quit concentrating on me—it's a useless cycle, and I only depress myself.* So, Cole contemplated on other things. The Christmas play, Skyler, and the world in general. When Scott asked where he wanted to be dropped off, Cole felt much better.

"Might as well go home first," he told Scott. Something still bothered Cole. He had to ask Scott the burning question before he lost courage.

Scott stopped by the house and started to get out. Cole stopped him. "Umm, Scott? May I ask you a question?"

"Sure." Scott closed the door again.

"Suppose there was a lady," Cole began slowly. "And suppose she took care of her nephew. They lived in a little house in town, just the two of them, for a number of years. Then one day the lady started seeing a special friend. This went on for awhile, and eventually there was a wedding. The question is this. Would the husband still want the nephew living with them?" Now that it was out in words, his concern almost seemed silly, but he was still glad he had asked. Cole twisted his fingers into a knot and refused to look at Scott.

"A good hypothetical question." Scott voice held understanding. "And the answer is an unmistakable yes!"

CHAPTER NINE

Kelsi, wearing what she called her "Narrator dress," pulled the curtains back to reveal the stage. The audience sat in expectant silence. Kelsi smiled and started speaking. "There might have been no church had not the Reverend James McKenzie come just when it seemed tottering to fall!"

At the end of the sentence she stopped, and Cole entered the stage, dressed in his Sunday best. "Good evening, friends," he began, sounding in control but not feeling it. Cole hadn't realized he could come this close to stage fright. "Welcome to *The Carols of Bethlehem Centre* play. We're glad you could come. After the play you are welcome to buy or donate for the fundraiser we are holding for Skyler, a five-year-old cancer patient at the North River Hospital. Thank you and enjoy your evening."

Kelsi continued. "There might have been no Sunday school had not Harold Thorton tended it as carefully as he tended his own orchard."

Doug came on stage, then left with Cole, holding a silent conversation. It took all of Cole's strength to keep from laughing. They rejoined the group backstage, where Tomika and Stephanie were giving last minute instructions to Chase, Lynn, Seth, and Kai.

"Remember," Tomika said. "All you boys have to do is follow Stephanie's directions."

Stephanie smiled. "Come on. It's our turn on stage." She led the way and they followed looking like an excited Sunday School class, which is what they were supposed to look like.

Scene one ended and Cole, Tyrell, and Doug rushed out onstage and, as quickly and noiselessly as possible, they pushed the correct props into position. Colton's job was to keep the audience occupied during the intervals.

"Must be a good entertainer," Cole remarked to Tyrell. "Everyone's laughing."

"Yeah," Tyrell grinned. "I saw the list of things he planned on saying, and it would make anyone laugh."

The play progressed smoothly. It wasn't professional, but that made it fun. When the curtains closed for the final time, the audience erupted with clapping. Pastor Jordan said a few words and dismissed everyone with a closing prayer.

The actors left the stage. Kelsi headed for the water fountain and Doug started for the fundraising table. Cole, Tyrell, and Colton followed.

"I gotta see this picture," Doug said over his shoulder to Tyrell.

Tyrell grinned at Cole. "Yeah, I know. Skyler's smile is pretty cute. Makes you cheer up just looking at him, which is why you should take a look."

"I appreciate your sense of humor," Doug replied. "Nice try to change the subject. Problem is my brain is in good working order tonight—I ate fish for dinner."

Tyrell's comeback was instant. "Thought something seemed fishy around here."

Doug brushed the poinsettia leaf away from the photo where Tyrell had artfully arranged it over his face. "Nice try. Hey, wow! I see Cole, I see Skyler and—hold on, is that a mummy?" He turned and studied Tyrell's face closely. "At least now it only looks like you got too close to your mom's sewing machine."

"You are too funny," Tyrell said.

Cole grinned. "What goes around, comes around." He was still smiling when someone touched his shoulder.

"Nice work with the play. It seemed almost real." Cole turned to see Scott and Aunt Sue—together.

"Um, thank you," Cole stammered. In the excitement of the evening all thoughts of Scott had fled to the farthest recess of his mind. Desperately, Cole searched for more words and came up empty.

Thankfully, Aunt Sue turned her attention to the bags of cookies and squares. Scott started a conversation with Tyrell, and Cole was left to regain his composure.

People started crowding around the table to see the photo of Skyler and to buy desserts. Cole slipped to the coat room where he could observe everyone without being observed himself.

The donations box, set beside the photo, received more attention than Cole had expected. Even Scott put his share in.

Tyrell found his cousin deep in thought three minutes later. "Hey, Cole, what's up?" He leaned against the wall next to Cole, and also surveyed the crowd. "A lot of people showed up tonight."

"Yeah, I'd say it was a good turnout." Cole watched Aunt Sue laugh at something Scott said. He felt a faint flicker of resentment and looked away.

"Did the fish bite well?" Tyrell asked.

Cole nodded. "It wasn't horrible. We only kept two though because the lake has a size limit."

"Too bad," Tyrell sympathized. "I assume you got to know Scott a little better?"

Cole thought back over their day. Sure, there were things he wanted to erase, but everything considered, it had been a good day. Best of all the trip had ended on a good note. Scott's strong "yes" still resounded through him with joy-filled tones. Cole turned his attention back to Tyrell. "Yes, I'd say we did. I think I can accept the fact that he's probably here to stay. Well, maybe a little better, or at least I'm trying too."

"Good," Tyrell grinned. "I figured you'd see through it eventually."

"Wait," Cole held up his hand. "I said I'm *trying* to. There are still things I don't like, but I think I can honestly say I feel a little better about Scott. I just hope the feeling stays."

"I'll keep praying," Tyrell encouraged. "With school resuming next week, you'll be able to think about other things."

"Other than myself," Cole agreed. "Yeah, I'm looking forward to going back in that perspective. Have to work a bit harder on my History scores though."

Tyrell moaned. "Same here with Geometry. I didn't do so well on the last few tests."

Doug joined them. "What's the serious conversation about?"

"School," Cole and Tyrell said in unison.

"School?" Doug frowned. "I thought you'd be discussing when to visit Skyler."

"Should be," Cole said. "I had been thinking Friday, but maybe that doesn't work with everyone."

Doug nodded. "Plan for that and, if someone disagrees, we'll move on to plan B."

"Which at this point hasn't been planned," Cole laughed. "Aunt Sue wants to drive some of us, but we won't all be able to go together. We'll have to find someone else to drive unless Doug wants to chauffeur."

"Consider me at your service," Doug made a mock bow. "You know I'd never pass up the offer."

Cole grinned. "Didn't want you to feel obligated. Thanks a lot, by the way."

The boys stepped aside to let a young family into the coat room. "Looks like people are leaving already," Cole said. "Maybe we should stand closer to the table in case someone has questions."

"There's still quite a few people out there," Tyrell observed. He strained to see better. "Looks like most of the cookies are sold and a number of the squares. Too bad. I had my heart set on a snack tonight."

Doug had no pity. "Pay your five dollars, and you'll get it. This is a fundraiser, after all."

"I put my donation in already," Tyrell reminded him. "And if I decide Tomika's bag of cookies is worth five dollars, I'll pay."

When everyone had left, other than some of the parents, the young people counted the money the fundraiser had brought in. Tyrell set the last ten-dollar bill on the pile and whistled. "That's quite a sum. I never dreamed we'd do this well."

"Neither did I." Cole returned the money to the donation box. "Hey, Tyrell, is your dad still here?"

"I think so." Tyrell laid the photo down and set the plant directly on top.

Tomika responded immediately and removed the poinsettia. "You'll ruin the picture," she scolded lightly. "This one's for Skyler."

"Oops." Tyrell looked sheepish.

Cole grinned and set out to find Mr. Woods. His uncle was sweeping the floor and starting to close things down. Cole waited until he turned off the stage lights, then approached him. "Uncle Philip, may I ask a favor?"

Mr. Woods stopped sweeping. "Ask away."

"Do you mind taking the money and writing out a check for Skyler's family. I think that'll be the simplest way for us to get it to them."

"I can do that," Mr. Woods agreed. "Is there anything else you'd like me to do?"

Cole thought a moment, then shook his head. "If something comes up Tyrell can let you know. And thanks for everything." His eyes said more than his words.

* * *

The winter air hung thick with big lacey snowflakes. Cole closed the car door and walked with Tyrell, Tomika, and Aunt Sue toward the hospital. Doug and the others planned to meet them in the lobby once they arrived.

The lobby teamed with people. Christmas wreaths still hung in the gift shop, and a few volunteers wore red-and-white hats. There was a short line up in front of the fast-food restaurant, and Cole could smell coffee and doughnuts. He turned to Tyrell. "Did your dad send along the check? I forgot about it."

Tyrell pulled the paper from his pocket. "Dad didn't forget."

"Yes, but you did," Tomika reminded him. "You almost—"

Tyrell cut her off. "Hey, it wasn't my department. There comes Doug."

The group headed up to Skyler's room. Outside the door, Cole stopped them. "Let me go in first. It'll surprise him more if he doesn't see all of us at once."

Everyone agreed. Cole knocked lightly on the half-closed door as the others moved back a few steps. Almost instantly a woman with curly brown hair appeared. Her eyes smiled when she saw Cole. "Hi, are you Skyler's cookie friend?"

"That's me," Cole replied. "My name's Cole Greyson, and I assume you are Skyler's mother?"

"Mary Hamilton. A pleasure to meet you. Skyler talks so much about his cookie friend. He's sleeping now, but I'll wake him. He'd be very disappointed if he missed you." She hurried back into the room.

Cole leaned out into the hall and motioned Tyrell to come closer. "Address the check to Mary Hamilton. That's his mom."

Tyrell grabbed a forsaken pen off a nearby cart. "Will do."

When Cole entered the room, Skyler was sitting in the middle of the bed, smiling sleepily. "Hi," he said. "I was hoping you'd come."

"I brought a surprise," Cole said mysteriously.

"Really?" Skyler woke up a little more. "Is it more cookies?"

"No," Cole said. "Something much bigger."

Skyler's eyes widened. "Did you bring your friend that plays hockey? Is he still hurt?"

In answer, Cole called out the open door. "Come on in, everyone." Then he stepped back to enjoy Skyler's expression.

Tyrell entered first and everyone filed after him. Skyler's eyes got enormous, and his smile stretched nearly to his ears. He turned to Cole and exclaimed in wonder, "Are these all your friends?"

"We are your friends too," Tomika answered. "I'm so glad I can finally meet you."

Tyrell stepped up to the bed and shook Skyler's hand. "How is my little fan doing?"

Skyler beamed. "I'm nearly *hydrosteric*, I'm so happy."

Cole grinned at the unique wording and Skyler's mom said, "He means *hysterical*." Cole noticed her voice held a slight catch and her eyes sparkled with tears.

They visited with Skyler for over an hour. The little boy couldn't ask enough questions about each person. Finally, Aunt Sue suggested that maybe it was time to let Skyler rest. Cole agreed and nodded for Tyrell to proceed.

"Mrs. Hamilton," Tyrell began. "We also brought a gift for you."

"You shouldn't have," the lady exclaimed. "You've blessed me so much already just by making Skyler happy."

"The main reason we came was to give you this," Tyrell said. He presented the check, neatly folded in half. "Thought we could help out a little."

With trembling fingers, Mrs. Hamilton took the paper and slowly looked at it. A tear dropped into her lap, closely followed by two more. "Oh, thank you," she whispered. "I don't know what to say. God bless you all."

Tomika handed the framed photograph to Skyler. "Merry Christmas and Happy New Year, Skyler."

"Thank you," Skyler exclaimed. He looked worried. "Should I be crying too?"

Cole laughed. "Only if they are happy tears." As the group left the room, he heard Skyler's mom whisper over and over. "I can't believe this. I just can't."

* * *

The days slipped by. School kept Cole occupied and since Scott was busy with work, he stayed in touch with Aunt Sue, mainly by phone call and email.

Life has nearly gone back to normal, Cole thought happily, one morning in January. *It's almost as though Scott was never in the picture.* The thought was pleasant. *I can like Scott this way. Maybe it will be easier than I thought.*

Aunt Sue's birthday fell on the last Thursday in January. Cole started planning a birthday surprise a week early. The awaited morning dawned, overcast and snowy. Cole hurriedly dressed for school and rushed downstairs. "Happy birthday, Aunt Sue," he greeted her.

"Thank you and good morning," Aunt Sue smiled. "Coffee's ready if you'd like some."

Cole waited till after breakfast to let Aunt Sue in on his surprise. When the dishes were put away, he said, "Tonight, after work, I want you to come home and put your feet up. I'll make supper, so don't worry about anything. I have it all planned."

Instead of looking pleased, Aunt Sue wilted. "Oh, Cole. I'm sorry. I should have told you sooner that I have other plans."

Cole's heart sank. "You do?"

"Yes," Aunt Sue said slowly. "Scott's taking me out for supper."

CHAPTER TEN

Cole kicked his locker door shut. It banged rather loudly in the near-empty hallway. Most of the pupils had already gathered for Morning Assembly, and Cole was running late. At that moment, he couldn't have cared less. Nothing sparked his interest other than seeing Scott banished to some deserted island on the other side of the world. *I had everything planned,* Cole agonized bitterly. *And then Scott showed up—AGAIN.*

The locker door refused to latch and swung slowly back open. Cole's firmly established scowl deepened. "Stupid door," he muttered, pulling his foot back to deliver another not-so-gentle kick.

A voice, close at hand, stopped him. "Well, at least I won't be the only one arriving last minute. How are you this morning, Cole?"

Cole spun around to face Mr. Bradburn, the school principal. "I'm surviving," he mumbled, turning back to his locker. If *surviving* sounded enough like *fantastic* maybe Mr. Bradburn wouldn't ask what was wrong. Then again, he probably would for sure.

Fantastic wasn't a word Cole used regularly. Nor was *surviving.*

Mr. Bradburn kept walking. "You have one minute, Cole." Punctuality ranked high on his list of good habits, and he expected the students to be on time.

Cole tried to feel relieved, but instead he felt disappointed. *Maybe I should talk to Mr. Bradburn.* Cole had a deep respect for his principal. Mr. Bradburn took time for his students, and Cole sometimes marveled at his patience. He made everyone feel secure and somehow brought out the best in the worst. His character had been Cole's role model ever since he had met him.

This time the locker door remained closed. *Probably because I didn't kick it.* Cole made it to Morning Assembly with twenty-five seconds to spare. Grabbing a songbook from the shelf, he headed for the back row and found an empty chair in the far corner.

Usually, the students who tried to get away with whispering claimed the back row. Since Cole rarely had a desire to whisper during devotions, the back row was never his first choice. Especially today Cole had nothing to say. Singing was difficult when the song leader chose "Does Jesus Care." In the struggle to control his emotion, Cole knew why he had chosen the back row.

The boy beside him was too busy sending silent messages to his friend to notice the single tear that escaped. That tear upset Cole. *How embarrassing! A fifteen-year-old crying in school.* Somehow it felt safer to be mad. Cole folded his arms and glared in the general direction of the podium.

The singing was over, and the devotional speaker, Lance Mitchell, was arranging his notes. Lance was in the grade ahead of Cole, but the two boys knew each other quite well. At that moment, Cole didn't care if he scowled at one of his best friends.

Lance read a short story about a man who carried everything he came across with him. The load grew heavier and heavier, but the man refused help.

That's me, Cole thought. He stopped scowling and listened attentively, but the story ended there. *How depressing, Lance.*

Lance scanned over the listeners. "How many of you think the story should end on that note?"

No one moved.

"How many of you think there should be a solution to this poor man's problem?"

A wave of hands went up all over the room.

"Anyone care to express their opinion?"

Tyrell stood up. "I think he should quit worrying about hurting his pride and get help. Anyone who insists on carrying all that invisible baggage along is going to work themselves into the grave."

"Good point," Lance nodded. "He needs to stop thinking he's strong enough on his own," he paused thoughtfully, "which is exactly what we like to think."

Cole mentally thanked Tyrell for not turning around to look at him.

Lance paged through his Bible. "Let me read you the answer to this man's problem. In Matthew 11, the last three verses, Jesus says, 'Come unto me all ye that labor and are heavy laden, and I will give you rest. Take my yoke upon you and learn of me, for I am meek and lowly in heart, and ye shall find rest unto your souls. For my yoke is easy, and my burden is light.'"

Cole concentrated on the tops of his shoes, not bothering to look up the reference. He knew it by memory. *But I've prayed about my problem! Wasn't I sincere enough?*

"Let me repeat the first part," Lance continued. "'Come unto me all ye that labor.' In other words, come unto me everyone who is discouraged, everyone who is sick of life the way it is at the present, everyone who can't find answers to their questions."

Cole shifted uncomfortably. Lance's paraphrased version hit close to home. *How can I find answers?* Cole's heart cried. *I've prayed, I've read Scripture references—what else should I do?*

Unknowingly, Lance touched on the very subject Cole wrestled with. "Does anyone have ideas on how we can find God's answers to our questions?"

Most of the students mentioned prayer and Bible reading. Once again Tyrell gave his opinion, and for the first time Cole saw the sense of it clearly. "I feel that God sometimes answers our questions though the advice of others."

After that Cole heard nothing else. He went through the motions of morning classes but didn't learn anything. Three times a teacher had to remind him to pay attention. Cole tried to concentrate on the lessons before him, but his thoughts always returned to the same pattern. *Talk to someone. God answers our questions through the advice of others. Talk to someone.*

At lunch period, Cole distractedly filled his tray, but made sure he avoided Tyrell's table. He set his tray down at a table in the corner. The boy at across from Cole only gave him a quick glance, before dropping his gaze to his phone. Thankfully, he could eat unnoticed here.

Once again Cole underestimated his cousin. Almost immediately, Tyrell approached him. "Hey, Cole. Are you feeling okay?"

Cole said nothing and took a bite of his hotdog. The boy across the table never looked up.

Tyrell persisted. "Why aren't you eating with us? Did I offend you somehow, or—" his voice dropped as a sudden thought hit him. "Or is it Scott?"

Suddenly upset with Tyrell's questions, Cole gripped the edge of the cafeteria table, and his fingers sank into somebody's forgotten wad of chewed gum. The last straw broke. Cole jumped up and tried to suppress the anger in his voice. "I'm not okay, and it's all Scott's fault. As usual!" He stormed off, not even noticing the startled look shared by Tyrell and his table companion.

When Cole could see clearly again, he found himself outside Mr. Bradburn's office, staring at the closed door. *Knock and it shall be opened unto you.* Where the verse came from, Cole didn't know, but it sounded great. He knocked, and Mr. Bradburn opened the door.

"Do you want something?" His words were deep and encouraging.

Cole tried to swallow. "I need to talk," he said in a barely audible voice. "Do you have time?"

"Definitely." Mr. Bradburn swung the door wide. "Come in." He went back to his desk.

Cole entered the office and closed the door. He stood there in silence, not sure how to begin. *Will he even understand? What if I'm just making a fool out of myself?*

"What brings you here?" Mr. Bradburn prompted.

Without much thought, Cole said the first thing that came to mind. "Chewing gum."

"Chewing gum?" Mr. Bradburn couldn't keep the surprise out of his voice.

Once Cole started talking he found it hard to stop. "Yes, chewing gum. You see, I was thinking about what Lance said this morning, and ever since my aunt started dating I've been mad at Scott, and I can't accept him, and Tyrell's always asking me if I'm okay, and then I stuck my fingers in chewing gum under the cafeteria table, and I'm so sick of everything—I wish life would just go back to normal." Cole choked on the last word, ending his tirade. He sank into a nearby chair and covered his face with his hands. A few tears escaped, but this time instead of making him mad, they brought a sense of relief.

Mr. Bradburn came over and put his hand on Cole's shoulder. He stood there without speaking.

Eventually, Cole regained control of his emotions. He took a deep breath and blurted out his real question. "Doesn't God care?"

Mr. Bradburn was silent for a moment. When he spoke, his voice was reassuring. "Cole, don't ever think He doesn't. He sees the whole picture. That's the difference. God sees the whole picture, and we only see a fraction. Think about it for a moment. I'm sure there is something God brought into your life to show you He cares. Something that maybe made you happy amid your struggles."

At first, Cole couldn't think of anything. Then, slowly, the pieces started falling into place. "I actually can," he mused out loud. "Skyler, my friend at the hospital; the school hockey game; the church Christmas play and fundraiser."

"God moves in a mysterious way," Mr. Bradburn quoted. He walked over to his desk. "Let me show you something."

Cole took the small motto Mr. Bradburn handed him. He blinked a couple times to bring the words into focus. The motto read—*He hath made everything beautiful in His time.*

Cole read it once then again. Something that felt a lot like hope sprang into his heart. "So, you think there's a reason for Scott?"

"That's your aunt's boyfriend?" At Cole's nod, Mr. Bradburn continued. "Have you ever wished you knew your dad?"

"Yes," Cole said. Sudden understanding flashed across his face. "You think God sent Scott to take his place?"

"It's possible," Mr. Bradburn smiled. "Think of it as His gift to you."

"Oh." It was a new idea. Cole raised his eyes to Mr. Bradburn's. "I guess I didn't receive it very gratefully."

Mr. Bradburn didn't hesitate. "And that's where you find God's greatest gift. The gift of new beginnings."

Cole sat in silence for awhile pondering that thought, then stood up. "Thanks for explaining it. Things make more sense now."

"I'm glad I could help. When you have time, read Ecclesiastes 3, and here, take this." Mr. Bradburn handed Cole the motto. "I want you to have it."

Cole accepted the gift. "Thanks. It will be a good reminder." He read the verse again, this time aloud. "He hath made everything beautiful in His time."

* * *

Cole usually arrived home from school fifteen minutes before Aunt Sue left the bakery. While he waited for her, he studied the chapter Mr. Bradburn had recommended. *God's timing is best. I just wish I had talked with someone earlier. Though I have a feeling it will still be a challenge to think good things about Scott—mainly because I resented him for so long.* The front door banged open, and Cole hurried to greet Aunt Sue before he lost courage.

Aunt Sue got the first words in. "Oh, Cole. I feel awful about this."

"I want you to go with Scott." Cole broke in before she could say more. "I talked with Mr. Bradburn today, and he helped me see things in a clearer light. Can you forgive my bad attitude?"

"Of course, I forgive you," Aunt Sue said as her special smile spread across her face. "I understand that this change isn't easy for you, Cole, but I feel this God's will for my life—and for yours."

"Yeah, I do too," Cole stated. "It just took me a while. If God wants Scott to be my uncle, I want to accept it, even if it's hard at times."

Aunt Sue laid a hand on his arm. "Thank you, Cole," she said. "It means a lot to hear you say that. Anyway, Scott's going to be here in half an hour, so I'd better start getting ready. You're welcome to spend the evening with Tyrell." She turned to leave.

Cole stopped her. "Aunt Sue? There's something else I want to say. I should have said it a while ago, but I couldn't."

"What is it?" Aunt Sue gave him her full attention.

Cole smiled. "Aunt Sue—Merry Christmas!"

ACKNOWLEDGMENTS

A BIG THANK YOU . . . .

To my parents, for allowing me to pursue the dream I have had for many years. Thanks for the encouragement you shared and for your patience when my eyes were once again glazed over in thought. Not to mention all the things I forgot when my mind was fixed on Tyrell, Tomika, and Cole. I appreciate all you have done. Thanks.

To my siblings (Lori, Ryan, Justin, Robyn, and Derek) for listening to the very first rough drafts one page at a time and begging me to pick up my grey pencil and finish the book. Thank you for being staunch supporters the whole way through.

To the Inkcourage Workshop (Julia, Beulah, Rynelle, and Lorraine) and Joy Deschutter for giving helpful advice on what I should change to keep the story flowing smoothly and realistic.

To all my other friends who read the story and shared their opinions. I appreciate the time you took to do so.

To Pamela and Terry-Lynn of the Markstay–Warren Public Library. Your assistance on copyright questions and how to use certain Word features was very helpful. I wouldn't have gotten this far, so easily, without you.

To Elaine for sharing your opinion to my many questions, and for searching through library books after school with me as I tried to decide how I wanted to set up the Acknowledgments page.

To the Tyndale and CrossLink publishing companies for taking the time to share helpful websites with an amateur writer. Your kindness is greatly appreciated.

> *Now unto Him that is able to do exceeding abundantly above all that we ask or think, according to the power that worketh in us, Unto Him be glory in the church by Christ Jesus throughout all ages, world without end. AMEN. (Ephesians 3:20–21)*